Python High Performance Programming

Boost the performance of your Python programs
using advanced techniques

Gabriele Lanaro

[PACKT] open source*
PUBLISHING   community experience distilled

BIRMINGHAM - MUMBAI

Python High Performance Programming

First published: December 2013

Production Reference: 1171213

Published by Packt Publishing Ltd.
Livery Place
35 Livery Street
Birmingham B3 2PB, UK.

ISBN 978-1-78328-845-8

www.packtpub.com

Cover Image by Gagandeep Sharma (er.gagansharma@gmail.com)

Credits

Author

Gabriele Lanaro

Reviewers

Daniel Arbuckle

Mike Driscoll

Albert Lukaszewski

Acquisition Editors

Owen Roberts

Harsha Bharwani

Commissioning Editor

Shaon Basu

Technical Editors

Akashdeep Kundu

Faisal Siddiqui

Project Coordinator

Sherin Padayatty

Proofreader

Linda Morris

Indexer

Rekha Nair

Production Coordinators

Pooja Chiplunkar

Manu Joseph

Cover Work

Pooja Chiplunkar

About the Author

Gabriele Lanaro is a PhD student in Chemistry at the University of British Columbia, in the field of Molecular Simulation. He writes high performance Python code to analyze chemical systems in large-scale simulations. He is the creator of Chemlab—a high performance visualization software in Python—and emacs-for-python—a collection of emacs extensions that facilitate working with Python code in the emacs text editor. This book builds on his experience in writing scientific Python code for his research and personal projects.

I want to thank my parents for their huge, unconditional love and support. My gratitude cannot be expressed by words but I hope that I made them proud of me with this project.

I would also thank the Python community for producing and maintaining a massive quantity of high-quality resources made available for free. Their extraordinary supportive and compassionate attitude really fed my passion for this amazing technology.

A special thanks goes to Hessam Mehr for reviewing my drafts, testing the code and providing extremely valuable feedback. I would also like to thank my roommate Kaveh for being such an awesome friend and Na for bringing me chocolate bars during rough times.

About the Reviewers

Dr. Daniel Arbuckle is a published researcher in the fields of robotics and nanotechnology, as well as a professional Python programmer. He is the author of *Python Testing: Beginner's Guide* from *Packt Publishing* and one of the authors of *Morphogenetic Engineering* from *Springer-Verlag*.

Mike Driscoll has been programming in Python since Spring 2006. He enjoys writing about Python on his blog at http://www.blog.pythonlibrary.org/. Mike also occasionally writes for the Python Software Foundation, i-Programmer, and Developer Zone. He enjoys photography and reading a good book. Mike has also been a technical reviewer for Python 3 Object Oriented Programming, Python 2.6 Graphics Cookbook, and Tkinter GUI Application Development Hotshot.

> I would like to thank my beautiful wife, Evangeline, for always supporting me. I would also like to thank friends and family for all that they do to help me. And I would like to thank Jesus Christ for saving me.

Albert Lukaszewski is a software consultant and the author of *MySQL for Python*. He has programmed computers for nearly 30 years. He specializes in high-performance Python implementations of network and database services. He has designed and developed Python solutions for a wide array of industries including media, mobile, publishing, and cinema. He lives with his family in southeast Scotland.

www.PacktPub.com

Support files, eBooks, discount offers and more

You might want to visit www.PacktPub.com for support files and downloads related to your book.

Did you know that Packt offers eBook versions of every book published, with PDF and ePub files available? You can upgrade to the eBook version at www.PacktPub.com and as a print book customer, you are entitled to a discount on the eBook copy. Get in touch with us at service@packtpub.com for more details.

At www.PacktPub.com, you can also read a collection of free technical articles, sign up for a range of free newsletters and receive exclusive discounts and offers on Packt books and eBooks.

http://PacktLib.PacktPub.com

Do you need instant solutions to your IT questions? PacktLib is Packt's online digital book library. Here, you can access, read and search across Packt's entire library of books.

Why Subscribe?

- Fully searchable across every book published by Packt
- Copy and paste, print and bookmark content
- On demand and accessible via web browser

Free Access for Packt account holders

If you have an account with Packt at www.PacktPub.com, you can use this to access PacktLib today and view nine entirely free books. Simply use your login credentials for immediate access.

Table of Contents

Preface

Python is a programming language renowned for its simplicity, elegance, and the support of an outstanding community. Thanks to the impressive amount of high-quality third-party libraries, Python is used in many domains.

Low-level languages such as C, C++, and Fortran are usually preferred in performance-critical applications. Programs written in those languages perform extremely well, but are hard to write and maintain.

Python is an easier language to deal with and it can be used to quickly write complex applications. Thanks to its tight integration with C, Python is able to avoid the performance drop associated with dynamic languages. You can use blazing fast C extensions for performance-critical code and retain all the convenience of Python for the rest of your application.

In this book, you will learn, in a step-by-step method how to find and speedup the slow parts of your programs using basic and advanced techniques.

The style of the book is practical; every concept is explained and illustrated with examples. This book also addresses common mistakes and teaches how to avoid them. The tools used in this book are quite popular and battle-tested; you can be sure that they will stay relevant and well-supported in the future.

This book starts from the basics and builds on them, therefore, I suggest you to move through the chapters in order.

And don't forget to have fun!

What this book covers

Chapter 1, Benchmarking and Profiling shows you how to find the parts of your program that need optimization. We will use tools for different use cases and explain how to analyze and interpret profiling statistics.

Chapter 2, Fast Array Operations with NumPy is a guide to the NumPy package. NumPy is a framework for array calculations in Python. It comes with a clean and concise API, and efficient array operations.

Chapter 3, C Performance with Cython is a tutorial on Cython: a language that acts as a bridge between Python and C. Cython can be used to write code using a superset of the Python syntax and to compile it to obtain efficient C extensions.

Chapter 4, Parallel Processing is an introduction to parallel programming. In this chapter, you will learn how parallel programming is different from serial programming and how to parallelize simple problems. We will also explain how to use multiprocessing, `IPython.parallel` and `cython.parallel` to write code for multiple cores.

What you need for this book

This book requires a Python installation. The examples work for both Python 2.7 and Python 3.3 unless indicated otherwise.

In this book, we will make use of some popular Python packages:

- **NumPy** (Version 1.7.1 or later): This package is downloadable from the official website (`http://www.scipy.org/scipylib/download.html`) and available in most of the Linux distributions

- **Cython** (Version 0.19.1 or later): Installation instructions are present in the official website (`http://docs.cython.org/src/quickstart/install.html`); notice that you also need a C compiler, such as GCC (GNU Compiler Collection), to compile your C extensions

- **IPython** (Version 0.13.2 or later): Installation instructions are present in the official website (`http://ipython.org/install.html`)

The book was written and tested on Ubuntu 13.10. The examples will likely run on Mac OS X with little or no changes.

My suggestion for Windows users is to install the Anaconda Python distribution (`https://store.continuum.io/cshop/anaconda/`), which comes with a complete environment suitable for scientific programming.

A convenient alternative is to use the free service `wakari.io`: a cloud-based Linux and Python environment that includes the required packages with their tools and utilities. No setup is required.

In *Chapter 1, Benchmarking and Profiling*, we will use KCachegrind (`http://sourceforge.net/projects/kcachegrind/`), which is available for Linux. KCachegrind has also a port for Windows—QcacheGrind—which is also installable from source on Mac OS X.

Who this book is for

This book is for intermediate to advanced Python programmers who develop performance-critical applications. As most of the examples are taken from scientific applications, the book is a perfect match for scientists and engineers looking to speed up their numerical codes.

However, the scope of this book is broad and the concepts can be applied to any domain. Since the book addresses both basic and advanced topics, it contains useful information for programmers with different Python proficiency levels.

Conventions

In this book, you will find a number of styles of text that distinguish between different kinds of information. Here are some examples of these styles, and an explanation of their meaning.

Code words in text, database table names, folder names, filenames, file extensions, pathnames, dummy URLs, user input, and Twitter handles are shown as follows: "The `plot` function included in `matplotlib` can display our particles as points on a Cartesian grid and the `FuncAnimation` class can animate the evolution of our particles over time."

A block of code is set as follows:

```
from matplotlib import pyplot as plt
from matplotlib import animation

def visualize(simulator):

    X = [p.x for p in simulator.particles]
    Y = [p.y for p in simulator.particles]
```

When we wish to draw your attention to a particular part of a code block, the relevant lines or items are set in bold:

```
In [1]: import purepy
In [2]: %timeit purepy.loop()
100 loops, best of 3: 8.26 ms per loop
In [3]: %timeit purepy.comprehension()
100 loops, best of 3: 5.39 ms per loop
In [4]: %timeit purepy.generator()
100 loops, best of 3: 5.07 ms per loop
```

Any command-line input or output is written as follows:

```
$ time python simul.py # Performance Tuned

real    0m0.756s

user    0m0.714s

sys     0m0.036s
```

New terms and **important words** are shown in bold. Words that you see on the screen, in menus or dialog boxes, for example, appear in the text like this: "You can navigate to the **Call Graph** or the **Caller Map** tabs by double-clicking on the rectangles."

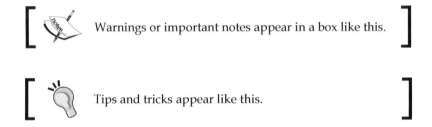

Warnings or important notes appear in a box like this.

Tips and tricks appear like this.

Reader feedback

Feedback from our readers is always welcome. Let us know what you think about this book—what you liked or may have disliked. Reader feedback is important for us to develop titles that you really get the most out of.

To send us general feedback, simply send an e-mail to feedback@packtpub.com, and mention the book title via the subject of your message.

If there is a topic that you have expertise in and you are interested in either writing or contributing to a book, see our author guide on www.packtpub.com/authors.

Customer support

Now that you are the proud owner of a Packt book, we have a number of things to help you to get the most from your purchase.

Downloading the example code

You can download the example code files for all Packt books you have purchased from your account at http://www.packtpub.com. If you purchased this book elsewhere, you can visit http://www.packtpub.com/support and register to have the files e-mailed directly to you.

Errata

Although we have taken every care to ensure the accuracy of our content, mistakes do happen. If you find a mistake in one of our books—maybe a mistake in the text or the code—we would be grateful if you would report this to us. By doing so, you can save other readers from frustration and help us improve subsequent versions of this book. If you find any errata, please report them by visiting http://www.packtpub. com/submit-errata, selecting your book, clicking on the **errata submission form** link, and entering the details of your errata. Once your errata are verified, your submission will be accepted and the errata will be uploaded on our website, or added to any list of existing errata, under the Errata section of that title. Any existing errata can be viewed by selecting your title from http://www.packtpub.com/support.

Piracy

Piracy of copyright material on the Internet is an ongoing problem across all media. At Packt, we take the protection of our copyright and licenses very seriously. If you come across any illegal copies of our works, in any form, on the Internet, please provide us with the location address or website name immediately so that we can pursue a remedy.

Please contact us at copyright@packtpub.com with a link to the suspected pirated material.

We appreciate your help in protecting our authors, and our ability to bring you valuable content.

Questions

You can contact us at questions@packtpub.com if you are having a problem with any aspect of the book, and we will do our best to address it.

Benchmarking and Profiling

1

Recognizing the slow parts of your program is the single most important task when it comes to speeding up your code. In most cases, the bottlenecks account for a very small fraction of the program. By specifically addressing those critical spots you can focus on the parts that need improvement without wasting time in micro-optimizations.

Profiling is the technique that allows us to pinpoint the bottlenecks. A **profiler** is a program that runs the code and observes how long each function takes to run, detecting the slow parts of the program. Python provides several tools to help us find those bottlenecks and navigate the performance metrics. In this chapter, we will learn how to use the standard `cProfile` module, `line_profiler` and `memory_profiler`. We will also learn how to interpret the profiling results using the program **KCachegrind**.

You may also want to assess the total execution time of your program and see how it is affected by your changes. We will learn how to write benchmarks and how to accurately time your programs.

Designing your application

When you are designing a performance-intensive program, the very first step is to write your code without having optimization in mind; quoting *Donald Knuth*:

> *Premature optimization is the root of all evil.*

In the early development stages, the design of the program can change quickly, requiring you to rewrite and reorganize big chunks of code. By testing different prototypes without bothering about optimizations, you learn more about your program, and this will help you make better design decisions.

The mantras that you should remember when optimizing your code, are as follows:

- **Make it run**: We have to get the software in a working state, and be sure that it produces the correct results. This phase serves to explore the problem that we are trying to solve and to spot major design issues in the early stages.

- **Make it right**: We want to make sure that the design of the program is solid. Refactoring should be done before attempting any performance optimization. This really helps separate the application into independent and cohesive units that are easier to maintain.

- **Make it fast**: Once our program is working and has a good design we want to optimize the parts of the program that are not fast enough. We may also want to optimize memory usage if that constitutes an issue.

In this section we will profile a test application—**a particle simulator**. The simulator is a program that takes some particles and evolves them over time according to a set of laws that we will establish. Those particles can either be abstract entities or correspond to physical objects. They can be, for example, billiard balls moving on a table, molecules in gas, stars moving through space, smoke particles, fluids in a chamber, and so on.

Those simulations are useful in fields such as Physics, Chemistry, and Astronomy, and the programs used to simulate physical systems are typically performance-intensive. In order to study realistic systems it's often necessary to simulate the highest possible number of bodies.

In our first example, we will simulate a system containing particles that constantly rotate around a central point at various speeds, like the hands of a clock.

The necessary information to run our simulation will be the starting positions of the particles, the speed, and the rotation direction. From these elements, we have to calculate the position of the particle in the next instant of time.

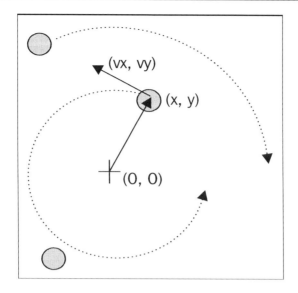

The basic feature of a circular motion is that the particles always move perpendicularly to the direction connecting the particle and the center, as shown in the preceding image. To move the particle we simply change the position by taking a series of very small steps in the direction of motion, as shown in the following figure:

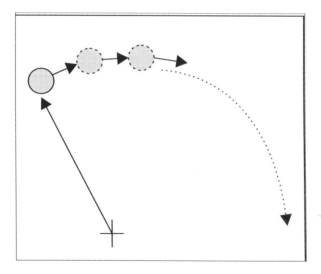

We will start by designing the application in an object-oriented way. According to our requirements, it is natural to have a generic `Particle` class that simply stores the particle position (x, y) and its angular speed:

```
class Particle:
    def __init__(self, x, y, ang_speed):
        self.x = x
        self.y = y
        self.ang_speed = ang_speed
```

Another class, called `ParticleSimulator` will encapsulate our laws of motion and will be responsible for changing the positions of the particles over time. The __ init__ method will store a list of `Particle` instances and the `evolve` method will change the particle positions according to our laws.

We want the particles to rotate around the point (x, y), which, here, is equal to $(0, 0)$, at constant speed. The direction of the particles will always be perpendicular to the direction from the center (refer to the first figure of this chapter). To find this vector

$$v = (v_x, v_y)$$

(corresponding to the Python variables v_x and v_y) it is sufficient to use these formulae:

$$v_x = -y/\sqrt{x^2+y^2}$$
$$v_y = x/\sqrt{x^2+y^2}$$

If we let one of our particles move, after a certain time *dt*, it will follow a circular path, reaching another position. To let the particle follow that trajectory we have to divide the time interval *dt* into very small time steps where the particle moves tangentially to the circle. The final result, is just an approximation of a circular motion and, in fact, it's similar to a polygon. The time steps should be very small, otherwise the particle trajectory will diverge quickly, as shown in the following figure:

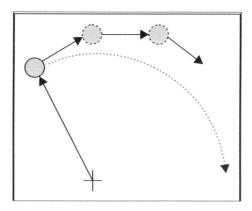

In a more schematic way, to calculate the particle position at time *dt* we have to carry out the following steps:

1. Calculate the direction of motion: v_x, v_y.

2. Calculate the displacement (d_x, d_y) which is the product of time and speed and follows the direction of motion.

3. Repeat steps 1 and 2 for enough time steps to cover the total time *dt*.

The following code shows the full ParticleSimulator implementation:

```python
class ParticleSimulator:

    def __init__(self, particles):
        self.particles = particles

    def evolve(self, dt):
        timestep = 0.00001
        nsteps = int(dt/timestep)

        for i in range(nsteps):
            for p in self.particles:

                # 1. calculate the direction
                norm = (p.x**2 + p.y**2)**0.5
                v_x = (-p.y)/norm
                v_y = p.x/norm

                # 2. calculate the displacement
                d_x = timestep * p.ang_speed * v_x
                d_y = timestep * p.ang_speed * v_y

                p.x += d_x
                p.y += d_y
                  # 3. repeat for all the time steps
```

We can use the `matplotlib` library to visualize our particles. This library is not included in the Python standard library. To install it, you can follow the instructions included in the official documentation at:

`http://matplotlib.org/users/installing.html`

 Alternatively, you can use the Anaconda Python distribution (`https://store.continuum.io/cshop/anaconda/`) that includes `matplotlib` and most of the other third-party packages used in this book. Anaconda is free and available for Linux, Windows, and Mac.

The `plot` function included in `matplotlib` can display our particles as points on a Cartesian grid and the `FuncAnimation` class can animate the evolution of our particles over time.

The `visualize` function accomplishes this by taking the particle simulator and displaying the trajectory in an animated plot.

The `visualize` function is structured as follows:

- Setup the axes and display the particles as points using the plot function
- Write an initialization function (`init`) and an update function (`animate`) that changes the *x*, *y* coordinates of the data points using the `line.set_data` method
- Create a `FuncAnimation` instance passing the functions and some parameters
- Run the animation with `plt.show()`

    The complete implementation of the visualize function is as follows:

    ```python
    from matplotlib import pyplot as plt
    from matplotlib import animation

    def visualize(simulator):

        X = [p.x for p in simulator.particles]
        Y = [p.y for p in simulator.particles]

        fig = plt.figure()
        ax = plt.subplot(111, aspect='equal')
        line, = ax.plot(X, Y, 'ro')

        # Axis limits
        plt.xlim(-1, 1)
        plt.ylim(-1, 1)
    ```

```
# It will be run when the animation starts
def init():
    line.set_data([], [])
    return line,

def animate(i):
    # We let the particle evolve for 0.1 time units
    simulator.evolve(0.01)
    X = [p.x for p in simulator.particles]
    Y = [p.y for p in simulator.particles]

    line.set_data(X, Y)
    return line,

# Call the animate function each 10 ms
anim = animation.FuncAnimation(fig, animate,
   init_func=init, blit=True,# Efficient animation
                               interval=10)
plt.show()
```

Finally, we define a small test function—`test_visualize`—that animates a system of three particles rotating in different directions. Note that the third particle completes a round three times faster than the others:

```
def test_visualize():
    particles = [Particle( 0.3,  0.5, +1),
                 Particle( 0.0, -0.5, -1),
                 Particle(-0.1, -0.4, +3)]

    simulator = ParticleSimulator(particles)
    visualize(simulator)

if __name__ == '__main__':
    test_visualize()
```

Writing tests and benchmarks

Now that we have a working simulator, we can start measuring our performance and tuning-up our code, so that our simulator can handle as many particles as possible. The first step in this process is to write a test and a benchmark.

We need a test that checks whether the results produced by the simulation are correct or not. In the optimization process we will rewrite the code to try different solutions; by doing so we may easily introduce bugs. Maintaining a solid test suite is essential to avoid wasting time on broken code.

Our test will take three particle and let the system evolve for 0.1 time units. We then compare our results, up to a certain precision, with those from a reference implementation:

```python
def test():
    particles = [Particle( 0.3,  0.5, +1),
                 Particle( 0.0, -0.5, -1),
                 Particle(-0.1, -0.4, +3)]

    simulator = ParticleSimulator(particles)

    simulator.evolve(0.1)

    p0, p1, p2 = particles

    def fequal(a, b):
        return abs(a - b) < 1e-5

    assert fequal(p0.x,  0.2102698450356825)
    assert fequal(p0.y,  0.5438635787296997)

    assert fequal(p1.x, -0.0993347660567358)
    assert fequal(p1.y, -0.4900342888538049)

    assert fequal(p2.x,  0.1913585038252641)
    assert fequal(p2.y, -0.3652272210744360)

if __name__ == '__main__':
    test()
```

We also want to write a benchmark that can measure the performance of our application. This will provide an indication of how much we have improved over the previous implementation.

In our benchmark we instantiate 100 `Particle` objects with random coordinates and angular velocity, and feed them to a `ParticleSimulator` class. We then let the system evolve for 0.1 time units:

```python
from random import uniform

def benchmark():
    particles = [Particle(uniform(-1.0, 1.0),
                          uniform(-1.0, 1.0),
                          uniform(-1.0, 1.0))
                 for i in range(1000)]

    simulator = ParticleSimulator(particles)
    simulator.evolve(0.1)

if __name__ == '__main__':
    benchmark()
```

Timing your benchmark

You can easily measure the execution time of any process from the command line by using the Unix `time` command:

```
$ time python simul.py
real    0m1.051s
user    0m1.022s
sys     0m0.028s
```

 The `time` command is not available for Windows, but can be found in the `cygwin` shell that you can download from the official website `http://www.cygwin.com/`.

By default, `time` shows three metrics:

*   `real`: The actual time spent in running the process from start to finish, as if it was measured by a human with a stopwatch
*   `user`: The cumulative time spent by all the CPUs during the computation
*   `sys`: The cumulative time spent by all the CPUs during system-related tasks such as memory allocation

Notice that sometimes `user` + `sys` might be greater than `real`, as multiple processors may work in parallel.

 `time` also offers several formatting options; for an overview you can explore its manual (by using the `man time` command). If you want a summary of all the metrics available, you can use the `-v` option.

The Unix `time` command is a good way to benchmark your program. To achieve a more accurate measurement, the benchmark should run long enough (in the order of seconds) so that the setup and tear-down of the process become small, compared to the execution time. The `user` metric is suitable as a monitor for the CPU performance, as the `real` metric includes also the time spent in other processes or waiting for I/O operations.

Another useful program to time Python scripts is the `timeit` module. This module runs a snippet of code in a loop for *n* times and measures the time taken. Then, it repeats this operation *r* times (by default the value of *r* is 3) and takes the best of those runs. Because of this procedure, `timeit` is suitable to accurately time small statements in isolation.

The `timeit` module can be used as a Python module, from the command line, or from **IPython**.

IPython is a Python shell designed for interactive usage. It boosts tab completion and many utilities to time, profile, and debug your code. We will make use of this shell to try out snippets throughout the book. The IPython shell accepts **magic commands**—statements that start with a `%` symbol—that enhance the shell with special behaviors. Commands that start with `%%` are called **cell magics**, and these commands can be applied on multi-line snippets (called **cells**).

IPython is available on most Linux distributions and is included in Anaconda. You can follow the installation instructions in the official documentation at:

```
http://ipython.org/install.html
```

You can use IPython as a regular Python shell (`ipython`) but it is also available in a Qt-based version (`ipython qtconsole`) and as a powerful browser-based interface (`ipython notebook`).

In IPython and command line interfaces it is possible to specify the number of loops or repetitions with the options `-n` and `-r`, otherwise they will be determined automatically. When invoking `timeit` from the command line, you can also give a setup code that will run before executing the statement in a loop.

In the following code we show how to use timeit from IPython, from the command line and as a Python module:

```
# IPython Interface
$ ipython
In [1]: from simul import benchmark
In [2]: %timeit benchmark()
1 loops, best of 3: 782 ms per loop

# Command Line Interface
$ python -m timeit -s 'from simul import benchmark' 'benchmark()'
10 loops, best of 3: 826 msec per loop

# Python Interface
# put this function into the simul.py script

import timeit
result = timeit.timeit('benchmark()',
                            setup='from __main__ import
                                benchmark', number=10)
# result is the time (in seconds) to run the whole loop
```

```
result = timeit.repeat('benchmark()', setup='from __main__ import
    benchmark', number=10, repeat=3)
# result is a list containing the time of each repetition
    (repeat=3 in this case)
```

Notice that while the command line and IPython interfaces are automatically determining a reasonable value for n, the Python interface requires you to explicitly pass it as the `number` argument.

Finding bottlenecks with cProfile

After assessing the execution time of the program we are ready to identify the parts of the code that need performance tuning. Those parts are typically quite small, compared to the size of the program.

Historically, there are three different profiling modules in Python's standard library:

- **The** `profile` **module**: This module is written in pure Python and adds a significant overhead to the program execution. Its presence in the standard library is due mainly to its extendibility.
- **The** `hotshot` **module**: A C module designed to minimize the profiling overhead. Its use is not recommended by the Python community and it is not available in Python 3.
- **The** `cProfile` **module**: The main profiling module, with an interface similar to `profile`. It has a small overhead and it is suitable as a general purpose profiler.

We will see how to use the cProfile module in two different ways:

- From the command line
- From IPython

In order to use `cProfile`, no change in the code is required, it can be executed directly on an existing Python script or function.

You can use `cProfile` from the command line in this way:

```
$ python -m cProfile simul.py
```

This will print a long output containing several profiling metrics. You can use the option `-s` to sort the output by a certain metric:

```
$ python -m cProfile -s tottime simul.py
```

You can save an output file in a format readable by the `stats` module and other tools by passing the `-o` option:

```
$ python -m cProfile -o prof.out simul.py
```

You can also profile interactively from IPython. The %prun magic command lets you profile a function using cProfile:

```
In [1]: from simul import benchmark
In [2]: %prun benchmark()
         707 function calls in 0.793 seconds

   Ordered by: internal time

   ncalls  tottime  percall  cumtime  percall
filename:lineno(function)
        1    0.792    0.792    0.792    0.792 simul.py:12(evolve)
        1    0.000    0.000    0.000    0.000
         simul.py:100(<listcomp>)
      300    0.000    0.000    0.000    0.000
         random.py:331(uniform)
      100    0.000    0.000    0.000    0.000 simul.py:2(__init__)
        1    0.000    0.000    0.793    0.793 {built-in method
             exec}
      300    0.000    0.000    0.000    0.000 {method 'random' of
          '_random.Random' objects}
        1    0.000    0.000    0.793    0.793
             simul.py:99(benchmark)
        1    0.000    0.000    0.793    0.793 <string>:1(<module>)
        1    0.000    0.000    0.000    0.000 simul.py:9(__init__)
        1    0.000    0.000    0.000    0.000 {method 'disable' of
 '_lsprof.Profiler' objects}
```

The cProfile output is divided into five columns:

- ncalls: The number of times the function was called.
- tottime: The total time spent in the function without taking into account the calls to other functions.
- cumtime: The time spent in the function including other function calls.
- percall: The time spent for a single call of the function—it can be obtained by dividing the total or cumulative time by the number of calls.
- filename:lineno: The filename and corresponding line number. This information is not present when calling C extensions modules.

The most important metric is tottime, the actual time spent in the function body excluding sub-calls. In our case, the largest portion of time is spent in the evolve function. We can imagine that the loop is the section of the code that needs performance tuning.

Analyzing data in a textual way can be daunting for big programs with a lot of calls and sub-calls. Some graphic tools aid the task by improving the navigation with an interactive interface.

KCachegrind is a GUI (Graphical User Interface) useful to analyze the profiling output of different programs.

> KCachegrind is available in Ubuntu 13.10 official repositories. The Qt port, QCacheGrind can be downloaded for Windows from the following web page:
>
> `http://sourceforge.net/projects/qcachegrindwin/`
>
> Mac users can compile QCacheGrind using Mac Ports (`http://www.macports.org/`) by following the instructions present in the blog post at this link:
>
> `http://blogs.perl.org/users/rurban/2013/04/install-kachegrind-on-macosx-with-ports.html`
>
> KCachegrind can't read directly the output files produced by `cProfile`. Luckily, the `pyprof2calltree` third-party Python module is able to convert the `cProfile` output file into a format readable by KCachegrind.
>
> You can install `pyprof2calltree` from source (`https://pypi.python.org/pypi/pyprof2calltree/`) or from the Python Package Index (`https://pypi.python.org/`).

To best show the KCachegrind features we will use another example with a more diversified structure. We define a recursive function `factorial`, and two other functions that use `factorial`, and they are `taylor_exp` and `taylor_sin`. They represent the polynomial coefficients of the Taylor approximations of `exp(x)` and `sin(x)`:

```python
def factorial(n):
    if n == 0:
        return 1.0
    else:
        return float(n) * factorial(n-1)

def taylor_exp(n):
    return [1.0/factorial(i) for i in range(n)]

def taylor_sin(n):
    res = []
    for i in range(n):
        if i % 2 == 1:
```

```
                    res.append((-1)**((i-1)/2)/float(factorial(i)))
            else:
                res.append(0.0)
        return res

    def benchmark():
        taylor_exp(500)
        taylor_sin(500)

    if __name__ == '__main__':
        benchmark()
```

We need to first generate the `cProfile` output file:

```
$ python -m cProfile -o prof.out taylor.py
```

Then, we can convert the output file with `pyprof2calltree` and launch KCachegrind:

```
$ pyprof2calltree -i prof.out -o prof.calltree
$ kcachegrind prof.calltree # or qcachegrind prof.calltree
```

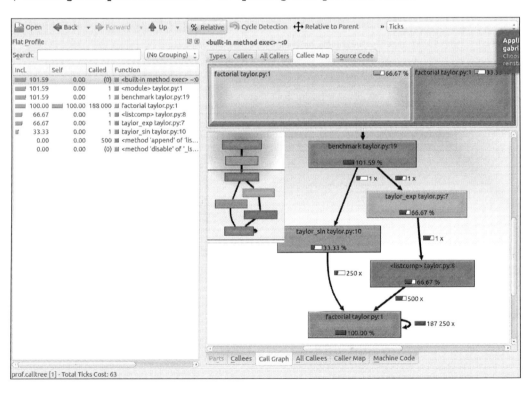

The preceding image is a screenshot of the KCachegrind user interface. On the left we have an output fairly similar to `cProfile`. The actual column names are slightly different: **Incl.** translates to `cProfile` module's `cumtime`; **Self** translates to `tottime`. The values are given in percentages by clicking on the **Relative** button on the menu bar. By clicking on the column headers you can sort by the corresponding property.

On the top right, a click on the **Callee Map** tab contains a diagram of the function costs. In the diagram, each function is represented by a rectangle and the time percentage spent by the function is proportional to the area of the rectangle. Rectangles can contain sub-rectangles that represent sub-calls to other functions. In this case, we can easily see that there are two rectangles for the `factorial` function. The one on the left corresponds to the calls made by `taylor_exp` and the one on the right to the calls made by `taylor_sin`.

On the bottom right, you can display another diagram—the call **graph**—by clicking on the **Call Graph** tab. A call graph is a graphical representation of the calling relationship between the functions: each square represents a function and the arrows imply a calling relationship. For example, `taylor_exp` calls <listcomp> (a list comprehension) which calls `factorial` **500** times `taylor_sin` calls factorial **250** times. KCachegrind also detects recursive calls: `factorial` calls itself **187250** times.

You can navigate to the **Call Graph** or the **Caller Map** tabs by double-clicking on the rectangles; the interface will update accordingly showing that the timing properties are relative to the selected function. For example, double-clicking on `taylor_exp` will cause the graph to change, showing only the `taylor_exp` contribution to the total cost.

> **Gprof2Dot** (`https://code.google.com/p/jrfonseca/wiki/Gprof2Dot`) is another popular tool used to produce call graphs. Starting from output files produced by one of the supported profilers, it will generate a `.dot` diagram representing the call graph.

Profile line by line with line_profiler

Now that we know which function we have to optimize, we can use the `line_profiler` module that shows us how time is spent in a line-by-line fashion. This is very useful in situations where it's difficult to determine which statements are costly. The `line_profiler` module is a third-party module that is available on the Python Package Index and can be installed by following the instructions on its website:

```
http://pythonhosted.org/line_profiler/
```

In order to use `line_profiler`, we need to apply a `@profile` decorator to the functions we intend to monitor. Notice that you don't have to import the `profile` function from another module, as it gets injected in the global namespace when running the profiling script `kernprof.py`. To produce profiling output for our program we need to add the `@profile` decorator to the `evolve` function:

```
@profile
def evolve:
    # code
```

The script `kernprof.py` will produce an output file and will print on standard output the result of the profiling. We should run the script with two options:

- `-l` to use the `line_profiler` function
- `-v` to immediately print the results on screen

```
$ kernprof.py -l -v simul.py
```

It is also possible to run the profiler in an IPython shell for interactive editing. You should first load the `line_profiler` extension that will provide the magic command `lprun`. By using that command you can avoid adding the `@profile` decorator.

```
In [1]: %load_ext line_profiler
In [2]: from simul import benchmark, ParticleSimulator
In [3]: %lprun -f ParticleSimulator.evolve benchmark()

Timer unit: 1e-06 s

File: simul.py
Function: evolve at line 12
Total time: 5.31684 s
```

Line #	Hits	Time	Per Hit	% Time	Line Contents
12					def evolve(self, dt):
13	1	9	9.0	0.0	timestep = 0.00001
14	1	4	4.0	0.0	nsteps = int(dt/timestep)
15					
16	10001	5837	0.6	0.1	for i in range(nsteps):
17	1010000	517504	0.5	9.7	for p

```
in self.particles:
    18
    19   1000000         963498      1.0      18.1
norm = (p.x**2 + p.y**2)**0.5
    20   1000000         621063      0.6      11.7
v_x = (-p.y)/norm
    21   1000000         577882      0.6      10.9
v_y = p.x/norm
    22
    23   1000000         672811      0.7      12.7
d_x = timestep * p.ang_speed * v_x
    24   1000000         685092      0.7      12.9
d_y = timestep * p.ang_speed * v_y
    25
    26   1000000         650802      0.7      12.2
p.x += d_x
    27   1000000         622337      0.6      11.7
p.y += d_y
```

The output is quite intuitive and is divided into columns:

- **Line number**: The number of the line that was run
- **Hits**: The number of times that line was run
- **Time**: The execution time of the line in microseconds (Time)
- **Per Hit**: Time divided by hits
- **% Time**: Fraction of the total time spent executing that line
- **Line Contents**: the source of the corresponding line

By looking at the percentage column we can have a pretty good idea of where the time is spent. In this case, there are a few statements in the `for` loop body with a cost of around 10-20 percent each.

Optimizing our code

Now that we have identified exactly how the time is spent, we can modify the code and assess the change in performance.

There are a few different ways to tune up our pure Python code. The way that usually produces the most remarkable results is to change the *algorithm*. In this case, instead of calculating the velocity and adding small steps, it would be more efficient (and correct, as it is not an approximation) to express the equations of motion in terms of radius `r` and angle `alpha` (instead of `x` and `y`), and then calculate the points on a circle using the equation:

```
x = r * cos(alpha)
y = r * sin(alpha)
```

Another way lies in minimizing the number of instructions. For example, we can pre-calculate the factor `timestep * p.ang_speed` that doesn't change with time. We can exchange the loop order (first we iterate on particles, then we iterate on time steps) and put the calculation of the factor outside of the loop on the particles.

The line by line profiling showed also that even simple assignment operations can take a considerable amount of time. For example, the following statement takes more than 10 percent of the total time:

```
v_x = (-p.y)/norm
```

Therefore, a way to optimize the loop is reducing the number of assignment operations. To do that, we can avoid intermediate variables by sacrificing readability and rewriting the expression in a single and slightly more complex statement (notice that the right-hand side gets evaluated completely before being assigned to the variables):

```
p.x, p.y = p.x - t_x_ang*p.y/norm, p.y + t_x_ang * p.x/norm
```

This leads to the following code:

```
def evolve_fast(self, dt):
    timestep = 0.00001
    nsteps = int(dt/timestep)

    # Loop order is changed
    for p in self.particles:
        t_x_ang = timestep * p.ang_speed
        for i in range(nsteps):
            norm = (p.x**2 + p.y**2)**0.5
            p.x, p.y = (p.x - t_x_ang * p.y/norm,
                        p.y + t_x_ang * p.x/norm)
```

After applying the changes we should make sure that the result is still the same, by running our test. We can then compare the execution times using our benchmark:

```
$ time python simul.py # Performance Tuned
real    0m0.756s
user    0m0.714s
sys     0m0.036s

$ time python simul.py # Original
real    0m0.863s
user    0m0.831s
sys     0m0.028s
```

By acting on pure Python we obtained just a modest increment in speed.

The dis module

Sometimes, it's not easy to evaluate how many operations a Python statement will take. In this section, we will explore Python internals to estimate the performance of Python statements. Python code gets converted to an intermediate representation—called **bytecode**—that gets executed by the Python virtual machine.

To help inspect how the code gets converted into bytecode we can use the Python module dis (disassemble). Its usage is really simple, it is sufficient to call the function dis.dis on the ParticleSimulator.evolve method:

```
import dis
from simul import ParticleSimulator
dis.dis(ParticleSimulator.evolve)
```

This will generate, for each line, a list of bytecode instructions. For example, the statement v_x = (-p.y)/norm is expanded in the following set of instructions:

```
20          85 LOAD_FAST               5 (p)
            88 LOAD_ATTR               4 (y)
            91 UNARY_NEGATIVE
            92 LOAD_FAST               6 (norm)
            95 BINARY_TRUE_DIVIDE
            96 STORE_FAST              7 (v_x)
```

LOAD_FAST loads a reference of the variable p onto the stack, LOAD_ATTR loads the y attribute of the item present on top of the stack. The other instructions (UNARY_NEGATIVE and BINARY_TRUE_DIVIDE) simply do arithmetic operations on top-of-stack items. Finally, the result is stored in v_x (STORE_FAST).

By analyzing the complete dis output we can see that the first version of the loop produces 51 bytecode instructions, while the second gets converted into 35 instructions.

The dis module helps discover how the statements get converted and serve mainly as an exploration and learning tool of the Python bytecode representation.

To improve our performance even further, we could keep trying to figure out other approaches to reduce the amount of instructions. It's clear however, that this approach has some limits and it is probably not the right tool for the job. In the next chapter, we will see how to speed up those kinds of calculations with the help of NumPy.

Profiling memory usage with memory_profiler

In some cases, memory usage constitutes an issue. For example, if we want to handle a huge number of particles we will have a memory overhead due to the creation of many `Particle` instances.

The module `memory_profiler` summarizes, in a way similar to `line_profiler`, the memory usage of the process.

> The `memory_profiler` package is also available on the Python Package Index. You should also install the `psutil` module (`https://code.google.com/p/psutil/`) as an optional dependency, it will make `memory_profiler` run considerably faster.

Just like `line_profiler`, `memory_profiler` also requires the instrumentation of the source code, by putting a `@profile` decorator on the function we intend to monitor. In our case, we want to analyze the function `benchmark`.

We can slightly change `benchmark` to instantiate a considerable amount (100000) of `Particle` instances and decrease the simulation time:

```
def benchmark_memory():
    particles = [Particle(uniform(-1.0, 1.0),
                          uniform(-1.0, 1.0),
                          uniform(-1.0, 1.0))
                 for i in range(100000)]

    simulator = ParticleSimulator(particles)
    simulator.evolve(0.001)
```

We can use `memory_profiler` from an IPython shell through the magic command `%mprun`:

```
In [1]: %load_ext memory_profiler
In [2]: from simul import benchmark_memory
In [3]: %mprun -f benchmark_memory benchmark_memory()
```

```
Line #    Mem usage     Increment    Line Contents
================================================
  135     45.5 MiB     0.0 MiB    def benchmark_memory():
  136     45.5 MiB     0.0 MiB       particles =
[Particle(uniform(-1.0, 1.0),
  137
uniform(-1.0, 1.0),
  138
uniform(-1.0, 1.0))
  139     71.2 MiB    25.7 MiB                          for i in
range(100000)]
  140
  141     71.2 MiB     0.0 MiB       simulator =
ParticleSimulator(particles)
  142     71.3 MiB     0.1 MiB       simulator.evolve(0.001)
```

 It is possible to run `memory_profiler` from the shell using the `mprof` run command after adding the `@profile` decorator.

From the output we can see that 100000 `Particle` objects take 25.7 **MiB** of memory.

 1 MiB (mebibyte) is equivalent to $1024^2 = 1,048,576$ bytes. It is different from 1 MB (*megabyte*), which is equivalent to $1000^2 = 1,000,000$ bytes.

We can use `__slots__` on the `Particle` class to reduce its memory footprint. This feature saves some memory by avoiding storing the variables of the instance in an internal dictionary. This optimization has a drawback: it prevents the addition of attributes other than the ones specified in `__slots__` (to use this feature in Python 2 you should make sure that you are using new-style classes):

```python
class Particle:
# class Particle(object):  # New-style class for Python 2

    __slots__ = ('x', 'y', 'ang_speed')

    def __init__(self, x, y, ang_speed):
        self.x = x
        self.y = y
        self.ang_speed = ang_speed
```

We can now re-run our benchmark:

```
In [1]: %load_ext memory_profiler
In [2]: from simul import benchmark_memory
In [3]: %mprun -f benchmark_memory benchmark_memory()
```

```
Line #    Mem usage    Increment    Line Contents
================================================
   138     45.5 MiB      0.0 MiB     def benchmark_memory():
   139     45.5 MiB      0.0 MiB         particles =
[Particle(uniform(-1.0, 1.0),
   140
uniform(-1.0, 1.0),
   141
uniform(-1.0, 1.0))
   142     60.2 MiB     14.7 MiB                              for i in
range(100000)]
   143
   144     60.2 MiB      0.0 MiB         simulator =
ParticleSimulator(particles)
   145     60.3 MiB      0.1 MiB         simulator.evolve(0.001)
```

By rewriting the `Particle` class using `__slots__` we can save 11 MiB of memory.

Performance tuning tips for pure Python code

As a rule of thumb, when optimizing pure Python code, you should look at what is available in the standard library. The standard library contains clever algorithms for the most common data structures such as lists, dicts, and sets. Furthermore, a lot of standard library modules are implemented in C and have fast processing times. However, it's important to always time the different solutions—the outcomes are often unpredictable.

The `collections` module provides extra data containers that can efficiently handle some common operations. For example, you can use `deque` in place of a list when you need to pop items from the start and append new items at the end. The `collections` module also includes a `Counter` class that can be used to count repeated elements in an iterable object. Beware, that `Counter` can be slower than the equivalent code written with a standard loop over a dictionary:

```python
def counter_1():
    items = [random.randint(0, 10) for i in range(10000)]
    return Counter(items)

def counter_2():
    items = [random.randint(0, 10) for i in range(10000)]
    counter = {}
    for item in items:
        if item not in counter:
```

```
            counter[item] = 0
        else:
            counter[item] += 1
    return counter
```

You can put the code in a file named `purepy.py` and time it through IPython:

```
In [1]: import purepy
In [2]: %timeit purepy.counter_1()
100 loops, best of 3: 10.1 ms per loop
In [3]: %timeit purepy.counter_2()
100 loops, best of 3: 9.11 ms per loop
```

In general, list comprehension and generators should be preferred in place of explicit loops. Even if the speedup over a standard loop is modest, this is a good practice because it improves readability. We can see in the following example, that both list comprehension and generator expressions are faster than an explicit loop when combined with the function `sum`:

```
def loop():
    res = []
    for i in range(100000):
        res.append(i * i)
    return sum(res)

def comprehension():
    return sum([i * i for i in range(100000)])

def generator():
    return sum(i * i for i in range(100000))
```

We can add those functions to `purepy.py` and test with IPython:

```
In [1]: import purepy
In [2]: %timeit purepy.loop()
100 loops, best of 3: 8.26 ms per loop
In [3]: %timeit purepy.comprehension()
100 loops, best of 3: 5.39 ms per loop
In [4]: %timeit purepy.generator()
100 loops, best of 3: 5.07 ms per loop
```

The `bisect` module can help with fast insertion and retrieval of elements, while maintaining a sorted list.

Raw optimization of pure Python code is not very effective, unless there is a substantial algorithmic advantage. The second-best way to speed up your code is to use external libraries specifically designed for the purpose, such as `numpy`, or to write extensions modules in a more "down to the metal" language such as C with the help of **Cython**.

Summary

In this chapter, we introduced the basic principles of optimization and we applied those principles to our test application. The most important thing is identifying the bottlenecks in the application before editing the code. We saw how to write and time a benchmark using the `time` Unix command and the Python `timeit` module. We learned how to profile our application using `cProfile`, `line_profiler`, and `memory_profiler`, and how to analyze and navigate graphically the profiling data with KCachegrind. We surveyed some of the strategies to optimize pure Python code by leveraging the tools available in the standard library.

In the next chapter, we will see how to use `numpy` to dramatically speedup computations in an easy and convenient way.

2
Fast Array Operations with NumPy

NumPy is the *de facto* standard for scientific computing in Python. It extends Python with a flexible multidimensional array that allows fast mathematical calculations.

NumPy works as a framework that allows coding complex operations using a concise syntax. The multidimensional array (`numpy.ndarray`) is internally based on C arrays: in this way, the developer can easily interface NumPy with existing C and FORTRAN code. NumPy constitutes a bridge between Python and the legacy code written using those languages.

In this chapter, we will learn how to create and manipulate NumPy arrays. We will also explore the NumPy broadcasting feature to rewrite complex mathematical expressions in an efficient and succinct manner.

In the last few years a number of packages were developed to further increase the speed of NumPy. We will explore one of these packages, `numexpr`, that optimizes array expressions and takes advantage of multi-core architectures.

Getting started with NumPy

NumPy is founded around its multidimensional array object, `numpy.ndarray`. NumPy arrays are a collection of elements of the same data type; this fundamental restriction allows NumPy to pack the data in an efficient way. By storing the data in this way NumPy can handle arithmetic and mathematical operations at high speed.

Creating arrays

You can create NumPy arrays using the `numpy.array` function. It takes a list-like object (or another array) as input and, optionally, a string expressing its data type. You can interactively test the array creation using an IPython shell as follows:

```
In [1]: import numpy as np
In [2]: a = np.array([0, 1, 2])
```

Every NumPy array has a data type that can be accessed by the `dtype` attribute, as shown in the following code. In the following code example, `dtype` is a 64-bit integer:

```
In [3]: a.dtype
Out[3]: dtype('int64')
```

If we want those numbers to be treated as a `float` type of variable, we can either pass the `dtype` argument in the `np.array` function or cast the array to another data type using the `astype` method, as shown in the following code:

```
In [4]: a = np.array([1, 2, 3], dtype='float32')
In [5]: a.astype('float32')
Out[5]: array([ 0.,  1.,  2.], dtype=float32)
```

To create an array with two dimensions (an array of arrays) we can initialize the array using a nested sequence, shown as follows:

```
In [6]: a = np.array([[0, 1, 2], [3, 4, 5]])
In [7]: print(a)
Out[7]: [[0 1 2]
         [3 4 5]]
```

The array created in this way has two dimensions—**axes** in NumPy's jargon. Such an array is like a table that contains two rows and three columns. We can access the axes structure using the `ndarray.shape` attribute:

```
In [7]: a.shape
Out[7]: (2, 3)
```

Arrays can also be reshaped, only as long as the product of the shape dimensions is equal to the total number of elements in the array. For example, we can reshape an array containing 16 elements in the following ways: (2, 8), (4, 4), or (2, 2, 4). To reshape an array, we can either use the ndarray.reshape method or directly change the ndarray.shape attribute. The following code illustrates the use of the ndarray.reshape method:

```
In [7]: a = np.array([0, 1, 2, 3, 4, 5, 6, 7, 8,
                       9, 10, 11, 12, 13, 14, 15])
In [7]: a.shape
Out[7]: (16,)
In [8]: a.reshape(4, 4) # Equivalent: a.shape = (4, 4)
Out[8]:
array([[ 0,  1,  2,  3],
       [ 4,  5,  6,  7],
       [ 8,  9, 10, 11],
       [12, 13, 14, 15]])
```

Thanks to this property you are also free to add dimensions of size one. You can reshape an array with 16 elements to (16, 1), (1, 16), (16, 1, 1), and so on.

NumPy provides convenience functions, shown in the following code, to create arrays filled with zeros, filled with ones, or without an initialization value (*empty*—their actual value is meaningless and depends on the memory state). Those functions take the array shape as a tuple and optionally its dtype:

```
In [8]: np.zeros((3, 3))
In [9]: np.empty((3, 3))
In [10]: np.ones((3, 3), dtype='float32')
```

In our examples, we will use the numpy.random module to generate random floating point numbers in the (0, 1) interval. In the following code we use the np.random.rand function to generate an array of random numbers of shape (3, 3):

```
In [11]: np.random.rand(3, 3)
```

Sometimes, it is convenient to initialize arrays that have a similar shape to other arrays. Again, NumPy provides some handy functions for that purpose such as zeros_like, empty_like, and ones_like. These functions are as follows:

```
In [12]: np.zeros_like(a)
In [13]: np.empty_like(a)
In [14]: np.ones_like(a)
```

Accessing arrays

The NumPy array interface is, on a shallow level, similar to Python lists. They can be indexed using integers, and can also be iterated using a `for` loop. The following code shows how to index and iterate an array:

```
In [15]: A = np.array([0, 1, 2, 3, 4, 5, 6, 7, 8])
In [16]: A[0]
Out[16]: 0
In [17]: [a for a in A]
Out[17]: [0, 1, 2, 3, 4, 5, 6, 7, 8]
```

It is also possible to index an array in multiple dimensions. If we take a (3, 3) array (an array containing 3 triplets) and we index the first element, we obtain the first triplet shown as follows:

```
In [18]: A = np.array([[0, 1, 2], [3, 4, 5], [6, 7, 8]])
In [19]: A[0]
Out[19]: array([0, 1, 2])
```

We can index the triplet again by adding the other index separated by a comma. To get the second element of the first triplet we can index using [0, 1], as shown in the following code:

```
In [20]: A[0, 1]
Out[20]: 1
```

NumPy allows you to slice arrays in single and multiple dimensions. If we index on the first dimension we will get a collection of triplets shown as follows:

```
In [21]: A[0:2]
Out[21]: array([[0, 1, 2],
                [3, 4, 5]])
```

If we slice the array with [0:2]. for every selected triplet we extract the first two elements, resulting in a (2, 2) array shown in the following code:

```
In [22]: A[0:2, 0:2]
Out[22]: array([[0, 1],
                [3, 4]])
```

Intuitively, you can update values in the array by using both numerical indexes and slices. The syntax is as follows:

```
In [23]: A[0, 1] = 8
In [24]: A[0:2, 0:2] = [[1, 1], [1, 1]]
```

Indexing with the slicing syntax is fast because it doesn't make copies of the array. In NumPy terminology it returns a *view* over the same memory area. If we take a slice of the original array and then change one of its values; the original array will be updated as well. The following code illustrates an example of the same:

```
In [25]: a = np.array([1, 1, 1, 1])
In [26]: a_view = a[0:2]
In [27]: a_view[0] = 2
In [28]: print(a)
Out[28]: [2 1 1 1]
```

We can take a look at another example that shows how the slicing syntax can be used in a real-world scenario. We define an array r_i, shown in the following line of code, which contains a set of 10 coordinates (x, y); its shape will be (10, 2):

```
In [29]: r_i = np.random.rand(10, 2)
```

A typical operation is extracting the x component of each coordinate. In other words, you want to extract the items [0, 0], [1, 0], [2, 0], and so on, resulting in an array with shape (10,). It is helpful to think that the first index is *moving* while the second one is *fixed* (at 0). With this in mind, we will slice every index on the first axis (the moving one) and take the first element (the fixed one) on the second axis, as shown in the following line of code:

```
In [30]: x_i = r_i[:, 0]
```

On the other hand, the following expression of code will keep the first index fixed and the second index moving, giving the first (x, y) coordinate:

```
In [31]: r_0 = r_i[0, :]
```

Slicing all the indexes over the last axis is optional; using r_i[0] has the same effect as r_i[0, :].

NumPy allows to index an array by using another NumPy array made of either integer or Boolean values—a feature called *fancy indexing*.

If you index with an array of integers, NumPy will interpret the integers as indexes and will return an array containing their corresponding values. If we index an array containing 10 elements with [0, 2, 3], we obtain an array of size 3 containing the elements at positions 0, 2 and 3. The following code gives us an illustration of this concept:

```
In [32]: a = np.array([9, 8, 7, 6, 5, 4, 3, 2, 1, 0])
In [33]: idx = np.array([0, 2, 3])
In [34]: a[idx]
Out[34]: array([9, 7, 6])
```

You can use fancy indexing on multiple dimensions by passing an array for each dimension. If we want to extract the elements [0, 2] and [1, 3] we have to pack all the indexes acting on the first axis in one array, and the ones acting on the second axis in another. This can be seen in the following code:

```
In [35]: a = np.array([[0, 1, 2], [3, 4, 5],
                       [6, 7, 8], [9, 10, 11]])
In [36]: idx1 = np.array([0, 1])
In [37]: idx2 = np.array([2, 3])
In [38]: a[idx1, idx2]
```

You can also use normal lists as index arrays, but not tuples. For example the following two statements are equivalent:

```
>>> a[np.array([0, 1])] # is equivalent to
>>> a[[0, 1]]
```

However, if you use a tuple, NumPy will interpret the following statement as an index on multiple dimensions:

```
>>> a[(0, 1)] # is equivalent to
>>> a[0, 1]
```

The index arrays are not required to be one-dimensional; we can extract elements from the original array in any shape. For example we can select elements from the original array to form a (2, 2) array shown as follows:

```
In [39]: idx1 = [[0, 1], [3, 2]]
In [40]: idx2 = [[0, 2], [1, 1]]
In [41]: a[idx1, idx2]
Out[41]: array([[ 0,  5],
                [10,  7]])
```

The array slicing and fancy indexing features can be combined. For example, this is useful if we want to swap the x and y columns in a coordinate array. In the following code, the first index will be running over all the elements (a slice), and for each of those we extract the element in position 1 (the y) first and then the one in position 0 (the x):

```
In [42]: r_i = np.random(10, 2)
In [43]: r_i[:, [0, 1]] = r_i[:, [1, 0]]
```

When the index array is a boolean there are slightly different rules. The Boolean array will act like a *mask*; every element corresponding to `True` will be extracted and put in the output array. This procedure is shown as follows:

```
In [44]: a = np.array([0, 1, 2, 3, 4, 5])
In [45]: mask = np.array([True, False, True, False, False, False])
In [46]: a[mask]
Out[46]: array([0, 2])
```

The same rules apply when dealing with multiple dimensions. Furthermore, if the index array has the same shape as the original array, the elements corresponding to `True` will be selected and put in the resulting array.

Indexing in NumPy is a reasonably fast operation. Anyway, when speed is critical, you can use the slightly faster `numpy.take` and `numpy.compress` functions to squeeze out a little more speed. The first argument of `numpy.take` is the array we want to operate on, and the second is the list of indexes we want to extract. The last argument is `axis`; if not provided, the indexes will act on the flattened array, otherwise they will act along the specified axis. The following code shows the use of `np.take` and its execution time compared to fancy indexing:

```
In [47]: r_i = np.random(100, 2)
In [48]: idx = np.arange(50) # integers 0 to 50
In [49]: %timeit np.take(r_i, idx, axis=0)
1000000 loops, best of 3: 962 ns per loop
In [50]: %timeit r_i[idx]
100000 loops, best of 3: 3.09 us per loop
```

The similar, but a faster way to index using Boolean arrays is `numpy.compress` which works in the same way as `numpy.take`. The use of `numpy.compress` is shown as follows:

```
In [51]: idx = np.ones(100, dtype='bool') # all True values
In [52]: %timeit np.compress(idx, r_i, axis=0)
1000000 loops, best of 3: 1.65 us per loop
In [53]: %timeit r_i[idx]
100000 loops, best of 3: 5.47 us per loop
```

Broadcasting

The true power of NumPy lies in its fast mathematical operations. The approach used by NumPy is to avoid stepping into Python by performing an element-wise calculation between matching arrays.

Whenever you do an arithmetic operation on two arrays (like a product), if the two operands have the same shape, the operation will be applied in an element-wise fashion. For example, upon multiplying two (2, 2) arrays, the operation will be done between pairs of corresponding elements, producing another (2, 2) array, as shown in the following code:

```
In [54]: A = np.array([[1, 2], [3, 4]])
In [55]: B = np.array([[5, 6], [7, 8]])
In [56]: A * B
Out[56]: array([[ 5, 12],
                [21, 32]])
```

If the shapes of the operand don't match, NumPy will attempt to match them using certain rules—a feature called *broadcasting*. If one of the operands is a single value, it will be applied to every element of the array, as shown in the following code:

```
In [57]: A * 2
Out[58]: array([[2, 4],
                [6, 8]])
```

If the operand is another array, NumPy will try to match the shapes starting from the last axis. For example, if we want to combine an array of shape (3, 2) with one of shape (2,), the second array is repeated three times to generate a (3, 2) array. The array is *broadcasted* to match the shape of the other operand, as shown in the following figure:

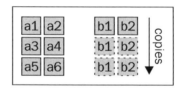

If the shapes mismatch, for example by combining an array (3, 2) with an array (2, 2), NumPy will throw an exception.

If one of the axes size is 1, the array will be repeated over this axis until the shapes match. To illustrate that point, if we have an array of the following shape:

```
5, 10, 2
```

and we want to broadcast it with an array (5, 1, 2), the array will be repeated on the second axis for 10 times which is shown as follows:

```
5, 10, 2
5,  1, 2 → repeated
- - - -
5, 10, 2
```

We have seen earlier, that we can freely reshape arrays to add axes of size 1. Using the numpy.newaxis constant while indexing will introduce an extra dimension. For instance, if we have a (5, 2) array and we want to combine it with one of shape (5, 10, 2), we could add an extra axis in the middle, as shown in the following code, to obtain a compatible (5, 1, 2) array:

```
In [59]: A = np.random.rand(5, 10, 2)
In [60]: B = np.random.rand(5, 2)
In [61]: A * B[:, np.newaxis, :]
```

This feature can be used, for example, to operate on all possible combinations of the two arrays. One of these applications is the *outer product*. If we have the following two arrays:

```
a = [a1, a2, a3]
b = [b1, b2, b3]
```

The outer product is a matrix containing the product of all the possible combinations (i, j) of the two array elements, as shown in the following code:

```
a x b = a1*b1, a1*b2, a1*b3
        a2*b1, a2*b2, a2*b3
        a3*b1, a3*b2, a3*b3
```

To calculate this using NumPy we will repeat the elements [a1, a2, a3] in one dimension, the elements [b1, b2, b3] in another dimension, and then take their product, as shown in the following figure:.

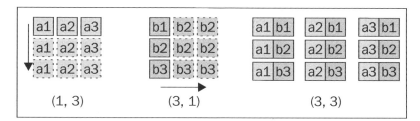

Our strategy will be to transform the array a from shape (3,) to shape (3, 1), and the array b from shape (3,) to shape (1, 3). The two arrays are broadcasted in the two dimensions and get multiplied together using the following code:

```
AB = a[:, np.newaxis] * b[np.newaxis, :]
```

This operation is very fast and extremely effective as it avoids Python loops and is able to process a high number of elements.

Mathematical operations

NumPy includes the most common mathematical operations available for broadcasting, by default, ranging from simple algebra to trigonometry, rounding, and logic. For instance, to take the square root of every element in the array we can use the `numpy.sqrt` function, as shown in the following code:

```
In [59]: np.sqrt(np.array([4, 9, 16]))
Out[59]: array([2., 3., 4.])
```

The comparison operators are extremely useful when trying to filter certain elements based on a condition. Imagine that we have an array of random numbers in the range [0, 1] and we want to extract the numbers greater than 0.5. We can use the > operator on the array; The result will be a boolean array, shown as follows:

```
In [60]: a = np.random.rand(5, 3)
In [61]: a > 0.5
Out[61]: array([[ True, False,  True],
                [ True,  True,  True],
                [False,  True,  True],
                [ True,  True, False],
                [ True,  True, False]], dtype=bool)
```

The resulting boolean array can then be reused as an index to retrieve the elements greater than 0.5, as shown in the following code:

```
In [62]: a[a > 0.5]
In [63]: print(a[a>0.5])
[ 0.9755  0.5977  0.8287  0.6214  0.5669  0.9553  0.5894
  0.7196  0.9200  0.5781  0.8281 ]
```

NumPy also implements methods such as `ndarray.sum`, which takes the sum of all the elements on an axis. If we have an array (5, 3), we can use the `ndarray.sum` method, as follows, to add elements on the first axis, the second axis, or over all the elements of the array:

```
In [64]: a = np.random.rand(5, 3)
In [65]: a.sum(axis=0)
Out[65]: array([ 2.7454,  2.5517,  2.0303])
In [66]: a.sum(axis=1)
Out[66]: array([ 1.7498,  1.2491,  1.8151,  1.9320,  0.5814])
In [67]: a.sum() # With no argument operates on flattened array
Out[67]: 7.3275
```

Notice that by summing the elements over an axis we eliminate that axis. From the previous example, the sum on the axis 0 produces a (3,) array while the sum on the axis 1 produces a (5,) array.

Calculating the Norm

We can review the basic concepts illustrated in this section by calculating the Norm of a set of coordinates. For a two-dimensional vector the norm is defined as:

```
norm = sqrt(x^2 + y^2)
```

Given an array of 10 coordinates (x, y) we want to find the Norm of each coordinate. We can calculate the norm by taking these steps:

1. Square the coordinates: obtaining an array which contains (x**2, y**2) elements.

2. Sum those using numpy.sum over the last axis.

3. Take the square root, element-wise, using numpy.sqrt.

The final expression can be compressed in a single line:

```
In [68]: r_i = np.random.rand(10, 2)
In [69]: norm = np.sqrt((r_i ** 2).sum(axis=1))
In [70]: print(norm)
[ 0.7314  0.9050  0.5063  0.2553  0.0778   0.9143
  1.3245  0.9486  1.010   1.0212]
```

Rewriting the particle simulator in NumPy

In this section, we will optimize our particle simulator by rewriting some parts of it in NumPy. From the profiling we did in *Chapter 1, Benchmarking and Profiling*, the slowest part of our program is the following loop contained in the ParticleSimulator.evolve method:

```
for i in range(nsteps):
  for p in self.particles:

    norm = (p.x**2 + p.y**2)**0.5
    v_x = (-p.y)/norm
    v_y = p.x/norm

    d_x = timestep * p.ang_speed * v_x
    d_y = timestep * p.ang_speed * v_y

    p.x += d_x
    p.y += d_y
```

We may notice that the body of the loop acts solely on the current particle. If we had an array containing the particle positions and angular speed, we could rewrite the loop using a broadcasted operation. In contrast, the loop over the time steps depends on the previous step and cannot be treated in a parallel fashion.

It's natural then, to store all the array coordinates in an array of shape (nparticles, 2) and the angular speed in an array of shape (nparticles,). We'll call those arrays `r_i` and `ang_speed_i` and initialize them using the following code:

```
r_i = np.array([[p.x, p.y] for p in self.particles])
ang_speed_i = np.array([p.ang_speed for p in self.particles])
```

The velocity direction, perpendicular to the vector (x, y), was defined as:

```
v_x = -y / norm
v_y = x / norm
```

The Norm can be calculated using the strategy illustrated in the *Calculating the Norm* section under the *Getting Started with NumPy* heading. The final expression is shown in the following line of code:

```
norm_i = ((r_i ** 2).sum(axis=1))**0.5
```

For the components (-y, x) we need first to swap the x and y columns in `r_i` and then multiply the first column by -1, as shown in the following code:

```
v_i = r_i[:, [1, 0]] / norm_i
v_i[:, 0] *= -1
```

To calculate the displacement we need to compute the product of `v_i`, `ang_speed_i`, and `timestep`. Since `ang_speed_i` is of shape (nparticles,) it needs a new axis in order to operate with `v_i` of shape (nparticles, 2). We will do that using `numpy.newaxis` constant as follows:

```
d_i = timestep * ang_speed_i[:, np.newaxis] * v_i
r_i += d_i
```

Outside the loop, we have to update the particle instances with the new coordinates x and y as follows:

```
for i, p in enumerate(self.particles):
    p.x, p.y = r_i[i]
```

To summarize, we will implement a method called `ParticleSimulator.`
`evolve_numpy` and benchmark it against the pure Python version, renamed
as `ParticleSimulator.evolve_python`. The complete `ParticleSimulator.`
`evolve_numpy` method is shown in the following code:

```
def evolve_numpy(self, dt):
    timestep = 0.00001
    nsteps = int(dt/timestep)

    r_i = np.array([[p.x, p.y] for p in self.particles])
    ang_speed_i = np.array([p.ang_speed for p in self.particles])

    for i in range(nsteps):

        norm_i = np.sqrt((r_i ** 2).sum(axis=1))
        v_i = r_i[:, [1, 0]]
        v_i[:, 0] *= -1
        v_i /= norm_i[:, np.newaxis]
        d_i = timestep * ang_speed_i[:, np.newaxis] * v_i
        r_i += d_i

        for i, p in enumerate(self.particles):
            p.x, p.y = r_i[i]
```

We also update the benchmark to conveniently change the number of particles and
the simulation method as follows:

```
def benchmark(npart=100, method='python'):
    particles = [Particle(uniform(-1.0, 1.0),
        uniform(-1.0, 1.0),
        uniform(-1.0, 1.0))
        for i in range(npart)]

    simulator = ParticleSimulator(particles)

    if method=='python':
        simulator.evolve_python(0.1)

    elif method == 'numpy':
        simulator.evolve_numpy(0.1)
```

We can run the updated benchmark in an IPython session as follows:

```
In [1]: from simul import benchmark
In [2]: %timeit benchmark(100, 'python')
1 loops, best of 3: 614 ms per loop
In [3]: %timeit benchmark(100, 'numpy')
1 loops, best of 3: 415 ms per loop
```

We have some improvement but it doesn't look like a huge speed boost. The power of NumPy is revealed when handling big arrays. If we increase the number of particles, we will notice a more significant performance boost. We can re-run the benchmark with a higher number of particles using the following code:

```
In [4]: %timeit benchmark(1000, 'python')
1 loops, best of 3: 6.13 s per loop
In [5]: %timeit benchmark(1000, 'numpy')
1 loops, best of 3: 852 ms per loop
```

The plot in the following figure was produced by running the benchmark with different particle numbers:

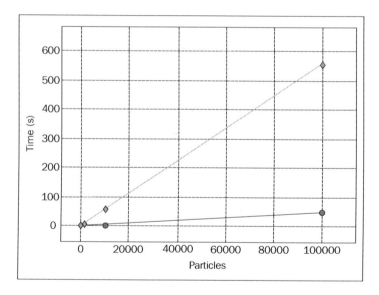

The plot shows that both implementations scale linearly with the particle size, but the runtime in the pure Python version (denoted with diamonds) grows much faster than the NumPy version (denoted with circles); at greater sizes we have a greater NumPy advantage. In general, when using NumPy you should try to pack things into large arrays and group the calculations by using the broadcasting feature.

Reaching optimal performance with numexpr

When handling complex expressions, NumPy stores intermediate results in the memory. David M. Cooke wrote a package called `numexpr` which optimizes and compiles array expressions on-the-fly. It works by optimizing the usage of the CPU cache and by taking advantage of multiple processors.

Its usage is generally straightforward and is based on a single function—`numexpr.evaluate`. The function takes a string containing an array expression as its first argument. The syntax is basically identical to that of NumPy. For example, we can calculate a simple `a + b * c` expression in the following way:

```
a = np.random.rand(10000)
b = np.random.rand(10000)
c = np.random.rand(10000)
d = ne.evaluate('a + b * c')
```

The `numexpr` package increases the performances in almost all cases, but to achieve a substantial advantage you should use it with large arrays. An application that involves a large array is the calculation of a *distance matrix*. In a particle system, a distance matrix contains all the possible distances between the particles. To calculate it, we should first calculate all the vectors connecting any two particles (i, j) defined as follows:

```
x_ij = x_j - x_i
y_ij = y_i - y_j
```

Then, we calculate the length of this vector by taking its Norm, as in the following code:

```
d_ij = sqrt(x_ij**2 + y_ij**2)
```

We can write this in NumPy by employing the usual broadcasting rules (the operation is similar to the outer product):

```
r = np.random.rand(10000, 2)
r_i = r[:, np.newaxis]
r_j = r[np.newaxis, :]
r_ij = r_j - r_i
```

Finally, we calculate the Norm over the last axis using the following line of code:

```
d_ij = np.sqrt((r_ij ** 2).sum(axis=2))
```

Rewriting the same expression using the `numexpr` syntax is extremely easy. The `numexpr` package doesn't support slicing in its array expression, therefore we first need to prepare the operands for broadcasting by adding an extra dimension as follows:

```
r = np.random(10000, 2)
r_i = r[:, np.newaxis]
r_j = r[np.newaxis, :]
```

At that point, we should try to pack as many operations as possible in a single expression to allow a significant optimization.

Most of the NumPy mathematical functions are also available in `numexpr`; however, there is a limitation. The reduction operations—the ones which reduce an axis, such as sum—have to happen last. So, we have to first calculate the sum, step out of `numexpr`, and calculate the square root in another expression. The `numexpr` code for those operations is as follows:

```
d_ij = ne.evaluate('sum((r_j - r_i)**2, 2)')
d_ij = ne.evaluate('sqrt(d_ij)')
```

The `numexpr` compiler will optimize memory usage by avoiding the storage of intermediate results and by taking advantage of multiple processors. In the `distance_matrix.py` file you will find two functions that implement the two versions of the distance matrix calculation: `distance_matrix_numpy` and `distance_matrix_numexpr`. We can import and benchmark them as follows:

```
from distance_matrix import (distance_matrix_numpy,
                             distance_matrix_numexpr)
%timeit distance_matrix_numpy(10000)
1 loops, best of 3: 3.56 s per loop
%timeit distance_matrix_numexpr(10000)
1 loops, best of 3: 858 ms per loop
```

By simply copying the expressions using `numexpr` we were able to obtain a 4.5x increase in performance in a real-world scenario over standard NumPy. The `numexpr` package can be used every time you need to optimize a NumPy expression that involves large arrays and complex operations, and you can do so with minimal changes in the code.

Summary

In this chapter, we learned how to manipulate NumPy arrays and how to write fast mathematical expressions using array broadcasting. This knowledge will help you to design better programs while obtaining massive performance gains. We also introduced the `numexpr` library to further increase the speed of our calculations with a minimal amount of effort.

NumPy works very well when handling independent sets of inputs, but it's not suitable when the expressions grow complex and cannot be split in element-wise operations. In such cases, we can leverage Python capabilities as a glue language by interfacing it with C using the Cython package.

3
C Performance with Cython

Cython is a language that extends Python by adding static typing to functions, variables, and classes. Cython combines the simplicity of Python and the efficiency of C. After rewriting your scripts in Cython you can compile them to C or C++, generating efficient code in a straightforward way.

Cython also acts as a bridge between Python and C, as it can be used to create interfaces to external C code. By creating bindings, you can reuse fast C routines in your scripts, effectively using Python as a glue language.

In this chapter we will learn:

- Cython syntax basics
- How to compile Cython programs
- How to use **static typing** to generate fast code
- How to efficiently manipulate arrays by making use of typed **memoryviews.**

Finally, we will apply our new Cython skills to profile and optimize the particle simulator.

While a minimum knowledge of C is helpful, this chapter focuses only on Cython in the context of Python optimization. Therefore, it doesn't require any C background.

Compiling Cython extensions

By design, the Cython syntax is a superset of Python. Cython can typically compile a Python module without requiring any change. Cython source files have the extension `.pyx` and they can be compiled to C using the `cython` command.

Our first Cython script will contain a simple function that prints *Hello, World!* to the output. Create a new file `hello.pyx` containing the following code:

```
def hello():
  print('Hello, World!')
```

The `cython` command will read `hello.pyx` and generate the `hello.c` file:

```
$ cython hello.pyx
```

To compile `hello.c` to a Python extension module we will use the gcc compiler. We need to add some Python-specific compilation options that depend on the operating system. On Ubuntu 13.10, with the default Python installation, you can use the following options to compile:

```
$ gcc -shared -pthread -fPIC -fwrapv -O2 -Wall -fno-strict-aliasing -
  lm -I/usr/include/python3.3/ -o hello.so hello.c
```

This will produce a file called `hello.so`: a C extension module importable from Python.

```
>>> import hello
>>> hello.hello()
Hello, World!
```

Cython accepts both Python 2 and Python 3 as input and output languages. In other words, you can compile a Python 3 `hello.pyx` file using the `-3` option:

```
$ cython -3 hello.pyx
```

The generated `hello.c` can be compiled without any changes to Python 2 and Python 3 by including the corresponding headers with the `-I` option in gcc as follows:

```
$ gcc -I/usr/include/python3.3 # ... other options
$ gcc -I/usr/include/python2.7 # ... other options
```

A Cython program can be compiled in a more straightforward way by using `distutils`—the standard Python packaging tool. By writing a `setup.py` script we can compile the `.pyx` file directly to an extension module. To compile our `hello.pyx` example we need to write a `setup.py` containing the following code:

```
from distutils.core import setup
from Cython.Build import cythonize

setup(
  name='Hello',
  ext_modules = cythonize('hello.pyx'),
)
```

In the first two lines of the previous code, we import the `setup` function and the `cythonize` helper. The `setup` function contains a few key-value pairs that tell `distutils` the name of the application and which extensions need to be built.

The `cythonize` helper takes either a string or a list of strings containing the Cython modules we want to compile. You can also use glob patterns using the following code:

```
cythonize(['hello.pyx', 'world.pyx', '*.pyx'])
```

To compile our extension module using `distutils` you can execute the `setup.py` script using the following code:

```
$ python setup.py build_ext --inplace
```

The `build_ext` option tells the script to build the extension modules indicated in `ext_modules`, and the `--inplace` option places the output `hello.so` file in the same location as the source file (instead of a build directory).

Cython modules can automatically be compiled using `pyximport`. By adding `pyximport.install()` at the beginning of your script (or issuing the command in your interpreter) you can import `.pyx` files directly; `pyximport` will transparently compile the corresponding Cython modules.

```
>>> import pyximport
>>> pyximport.install()
>>> import hello # This will compile hello.pyx
```

Unfortunately, `pyximport` will not work for all kinds of configurations (for example when they involve a combination of C and Cython files), but it comes in handy for testing simple scripts.

Since version 0.13, IPython includes the `cythonmagic` extension to interactively write and test a series of Cython statements. You can load the extensions in an IPython shell using `load_ext`:

```
In [1]: %load_ext cythonmagic
```

Once the extension is loaded you can use the `%%cython` *cell magic* to write a multi-line Cython snippet. In the following example, we define a `hello_snippet` function that will be compiled and added to the `session` namespace:

```
In [2]: %%cython
   ....:    def hello_snippet():
   ....:        print("Hello, Cython!")
   ....:
In [3]:  hello_snippet()
Hello,  Cython!
```

Adding static types

In Python, variables have an associated type that can change during the execution. While this feature is desirable, as it makes the language more flexible, the interpreter needs to do type-checks and method look-ups to correctly handle operations between variables—an extra step that introduces a significant overhead. Cython extends the Python language with static type declarations; in this way it can generate efficient C code by avoiding the Python interpreter.

The main way to declare data types in Cython is by using `cdef` statements. The `cdef` keyword can be used in multiple contexts: to declare variables, functions, and extension types (`cdef` classes).

Variables

In Cython you can declare the type of a variable by prepending the variable with `cdef` and its respective type. For example, we can declare the variable `i` as a 16 bit integer in the following way:

```
cdef int i
```

The `cdef` statement supports multiple variable names on the same line, along with optional initialization values, as seen in the following line of code:

```
cdef double a, b = 2.0, c = 3.0
```

Typed variables are treated differently in comparison to standard variables. In Python, variables are often regarded as *labels* referring to objects in memory. At any point in the program, we can assign a string to a variable as follows:

```
a = 'hello'
```

The string *hello* will be bound to the variable a. At a different place in the program, we can assign to the same variable another value, for example an integer:

```
a = 1
```

Python will assign the integer object *1* to the variable a without any problem.

Typed variables can be considered more like *data containers*; we *store* the value in the variable and only values of the same type are allowed to get in. For example, if we declare the variable a as an int type variable, and then we try to assign it to a double, Cython will trigger an error, as shown in the following code:

```
In [4]: %%cython
   ....: cdef int i
   ....: i = 3.0
   ....:
# Output has been cut
...cf4b.pyx:2:4 Cannot assign type 'double' to 'int'
```

Static typing allows useful optimizations. If we declare indexes to be used in a loop as integers, Cython will rewrite the loops in pure C without stepping into the Python interpreter. In the following example, we do an iteration 100 times and each time we increment the int variable j:

```
In [5]: %%cython
   ....: def example():
   ....:     cdef int i, j=0
   ....:     for i in range(100):
   ....:         j += 1
   ....:     return j
   ....:
In [6]: example()
Out[6]: 100
```

To understand how big the improvement is, we will compare the speed with an analogous, pure Python loop:

```
In [7]: def example_python():
   ....:     j=0
   ....:     for i in range(100):
   ....:         j += 1
   ....:     return j
   ....:
In [8]: %timeit example()
10000000 loops, best of 3: 25 ns per loop
In [9]: %timeit example_python()
100000 loops, best of 3: 2.74 us per loop
```

The speedup obtained by writing the loop with typing information is a whopping 100x! This works because the Cython loop has first been converted to pure C and then to efficient machine code, while the Python loop still relies on the slow interpreter.

We can declare a variable of any available C type, and we can also define custom types by using C structs, enums, and typedefs. An interesting example is that if we declare a variable to be of `object` type, the variable will accept any kind of Python object:

```
cdef object a_py
# both 'hello' and 1 are Python objects
a_py = 'hello'
a_py = 1
```

Sometimes, certain types of variables are compatible (such as `float` and `int` numbers) but not exactly the same. In Cython it is possible to convert (*cast*) between types by surrounding the destination type with < and > pointy brackets, as shown in the following code snippet:

```
cdef int a = 0
cdef double b
b = <double> a
```

Functions

You can add type information to the arguments of a Python function by specifying the type in front of the argument name. Such functions will work and perform like a regular Python function but its arguments will be type-checked. We can write a `max_python` function, which returns the greater value between two integers in the following way:

```
def max_python(int a, int b):
    return a if a > b else b
```

That function doesn't provide much benefit except for type-checking. To take advantage of Cython optimizations we have to declare the function using a `cdef` statement and an optional return type, as in the following code:

```
cdef int max_cython(int a, int b):
    return a if a > b else b
```

Functions declared in this way are translated to native C functions, which are not callable from Python. They have much less overhead compared to Python functions, and using them results in a substantial increase in performance. Their scope is restricted to the same Cython file, unless they're exposed in a definition file (refer to the *Sharing Declarations* section).

Cython allows you to define functions that are both callable from Python and translatable to native C functions. If you declare a function with the keyword `cpdef`, Cython will generate two versions of the function — a Python version available to the interpreter, and a fast C function usable from Cython — achieving both convenience and speed. The `cpdef` syntax is equivalent to `cdef`, shown as follows:

```
cpdef int max_hybrid(int a, int b):
  return a if a > b else b
```

Sometimes, the call overhead can be a performance issue even with C functions, especially when the same function is called many times in a critical loop. When the function body is small, it is convenient to add the `inline` keyword in front of the function definition; the function call will be removed and replaced by the function body. For instance, our following `max` function is a good candidate for *inlining*:

```
cdef inline int max_inline(int a, int b):
  return a if a > b else b
```

Classes

The `cdef` keyword can also be put in front of a class definition to create an *extension type*. An extension type is similar to a Python class but its attributes must have a type and are stored in an efficient C *struct*.

We can define an extension type by using the `cdef class` statement and declaring its attributes in the class body. For example, we can create an extension type `Point`, as shown in the following code, which stores two coordinates (x, y) of type `double`:

```
cdef class Point:
  cdef double x
  cdef double y

  def __init__(self, double x,double y):
    self.x = x
    self.y = y
```

Accessing the declared attributes in the class methods allows Cython to avoid the Python attribute look-up by replacing it with direct access to the `struct` fields. In this way, attribute access becomes an extremely fast operation.

To take advantage of the `struct` access, Cython needs to know that the variable is an extension type at the time of compilation. You can use the extension type name (such as `Point`) in any context where you would use a standard one (such as `double`, `float`, `int`). For example, if we want a Cython function that calculates the `norm` of a `Point`, we have to declare the input variable as `Point`, as shown in the following code:

```
cdef double norm(Point p):
    return p.x**2 + p.y**2
```

By default, access to the attributes is restricted to Cython code. If you try to access an extension type attribute from Python, you will get an `AttributeError` shown as follows:

```
>>> a = Point(0.0, 0.0)
>>> a.x
AttributeError: 'Point' object has no attribute 'x'
```

In order to access attributes from Python code you have to use the `public` (for read-write access) or `readonly` specifiers in the attribute declaration, as shown in the following code:

```
cdef class Point:
    cdef public double x
```

Extension types do not support the addition of extra attributes. A workaround for this problem is subclassing the extension type, creating a derived Python class.

Sharing declarations

When writing your Cython modules, you may want to encapsulate generic functions and types in a separate file. Cython allows you to reuse those components with the `cimport` statement by writing a *definition file*.

Let's say we have a module with the functions `max` and `min`, and we want to reuse those functions in multiple Cython programs. If we simply write a `.pyx` file — also called *implementation file* — the functions declared are confined in the same module.

 Definition files are also used to interface Cython with an external C code. The idea is to copy the types and function prototypes in the definition file and leave the implementation to the external C code.

To share those functions we need to write a definition file, with a `.pxd` extension. Such a file only contains the types and function prototypes that we want share to other modules—a *public* interface. We can write the prototypes of our `max` and `min` functions in a file named `mathlib.pxd` as follows:

```
cdef int max(int a, int b)
cdef int min(int a, int b)
```

As you can see, we only write the function name and arguments, without implementing the function body.

The function implementation goes into the implementation file with the same base name but `.pyx` extension—`mathlib.pyx`:

```
cdef int max(int a, int b):
   return a if a > b else b

cdef int min(int a, int b):
   return a if a < b else b
```

The `mathlib` module is now importable from another Cython module.

To test our Cython module we will create a file named `distance.pyx` containing a function named `chebyshev`. The function will calculate the Chebyshev distance between two points, as shown in the following code. The Chebyshev distance between two coordinates (x1, y1) and (x2, y2) is defined as the maximum value of the difference between each coordinate.

```
max(abs(x1 - x2), abs(y1 - y2))
```

To implement the `chebyshev` function we will use the `max` function, declared in `mathlib.pxd` by importing it with the `cimport` statement, as shown in the following code snippet:

```
from mathlib cimport max

def chebyshev(int x1,int y1,int x2,int y2):
   return max(abs(x1 - x2), abs(y1 - y2))
```

The `cimport` statement will read `hello.pxd` and the `max` definition will be used to generate the `distance.c` file.

Working with arrays

Numerical and high performance calculations often make use of arrays. Cython provides an easy way to interact with them, from the low-level approach of C arrays, to the more general *typed memoryviews*.

C arrays and pointers

C arrays are a collection of items of the same size stored contiguously in memory. Before digging into the details, it is helpful to understand (or review) how memory is managed in C.

Variables in C are like containers. When creating a variable, a space in memory is reserved to store its value. For example, if we create a variable containing a 64 bit floating point number (double), the program will allocate 64 bit (16 bytes) of memory. This portion of memory can be accessed through an address to that memory location.

To obtain the address of a variable we can use the *address operator*, denoted with the & symbol. We can also use the printf function, as follows, available in the libc.stdio Cython module to print the address of this variable:

```
In [1]: %%cython
   ...: cdef double a
   ...: from libc.stdio cimport printf
   ...: printf("%p", &a)
   ...:
0x7fc8bb611210
```

Memory addresses can be stored in special variables—*pointers*—declared by putting a * prefix on the variable name as follows:

```
from libc.stdio cimport printf
cdef double a
cdef double *a_pointer
a_pointer = &a # They are of the same data type
```

If we have a pointer and we want to grab the value contained in the address it's pointing at, we can use the *dereference operator*, denoted with the * symbol, as shown in the following code. Be careful, the * used in this context has a different meaning from the * used in the variable declaration.

```
cdef double a
cdef double *a_pointer
a_pointer = &a
a = 3.0
print(*a_pointer) # prints 3.0
```

When declaring a C array, the program allocates enough space to contain several elements of the specified size. For instance, to create an array that has 10 `double` values (8 bytes each), the program will reserve *8 * 10 = 80* bytes of contiguous space in memory. In Cython we can declare such an array using the following syntax:

```
cdef double arr[10]
```

We can also declare a multidimensional array, like an array with 5 rows and 2 columns using the following syntax:

```
cdef double arr[5][2]
```

The memory will be allocated in a single block of memory, row after row. This order is commonly referred to as *row-major* and is represented in the following figure. Arrays can also be ordered *column-mayor*, as it happens in the FORTRAN programming language.

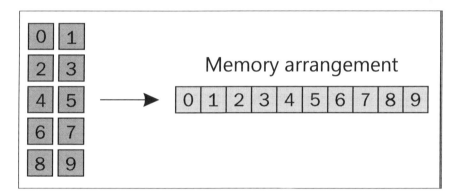

 Array ordering has important consequences. When iterating a C array over the last dimension, we access contiguous memory blocks (in our example 0, 1, 2, 3 ...)while when we iterate on the first dimension, we skip a few positions (0, 2, 4, 6, 8, 1 ...). You should always try to access memory contiguously as this optimizes cache usage.

We can store and retrieve elements from the array by using standard indexing, C arrays don't support fancy indexing or slices:

```
arr[0] = 1.0
```

C arrays can also be used as pointers. The `arr` variable, in fact, is a pointer to the first element of the array. We can verify that the address of the first element of the array is the same as the address contained in the variable `arr`:

```
In [1]: %%cython
   ...: from libc.stdio cimport printf
   ...: cdef double arr[10]
   ...: printf("%p\n", arr)
   ...: printf("%p\n", &arr[0])
   ...:
0x7ff6de204220
0x7ff6de204220
```

You should use C arrays and pointers when interfacing with existing C libraries or when you need a fine control over the memory. For more common use-cases you can employ NumPy arrays or typed memoryviews.

NumPy arrays

NumPy arrays can be used in Cython as normal Python objects, by using their already optimized broadcasted operations.

The problem comes when we want to efficiently iterate over the array. When we do an indexing operation on a NumPy array, a few other operations take place at the interpreter level causing a major overhead. Cython can optimize those indexing operations by acting directly on the underlying memory area used by NumPy arrays, allowing us to treat them just like C arrays.

NumPy array support comes in the form of a `ndarray` data type. We first have to `cimport` the `numpy` module. We assign it to the name `c_np` to differentiate it from the regular `numpy` Python module as follows:

```
cimport numpy as c_np
```

We can now declare a NumPy array by specifying the type of the array elements and the number of dimensions, with a special syntax called *buffer syntax*. To declare a two-dimensional array of type `double` we can use the following code:

```
cdef c_np.ndarray[double, ndim=2] arr
```

An array defined in this way will be indexed by acting directly on the underlying memory area; the operation will avoid the Python interpreter giving us a tremendous speed boost.

In the next example, we will show the usage of the buffer syntax and compare it with the normal Python version.

We first write the `numpy_bench_py` function that increments each element of `py_arr` by 1000. We declared the index `i` as integer so that we avoid the `for` loop overhead:

```
In [1]:  %%cython
   ...:  import numpy as np
   ...:  def numpy_bench_py():
   ...:      py_arr = np.random.rand(1000)
   ...:      cdef int i
   ...:      for i in range(1000):
   ...:          py_arr[i] += 1
```

Then we write the same function using the buffer syntax. Notice that after we define the `c_arr` variable using `c_np.ndarray`, we can assign to it an array from the numpy Python module:

```
In [2]:  %%cython
   ...:  import numpy as np
   ...:  cimport numpy as c_np
   ...:  def numpy_bench_c():
   ...:      cdef c_np.ndarray[double, ndim=1] c_arr
   ...:      c_arr = np.random.rand(1000)
   ...:      cdef int i
   ...:
   ...:      for i in range(1000):
   ...:          c_arr[i] += 1
```

We can time the results using `timeit`, obtaining an impressive 50x speedup:

```
In [10]: %timeit numpy_bench_c()
100000 loops, best of 3: 11.5 us per loop
In [11]: %timeit numpy_bench_py()
1000 loops, best of 3: 603 us per loop
```

Typed memoryviews

C and NumPy arrays are both objects that act on a memory area. Cython provides a universal object—the *typed memoryview*—to access arrays and other data structures that expose the so called *buffer interface*, such as the built-ins `bytes`, `bytearray`, and `array.array`.

A **memoryview** is an object that maintains a reference on a certain memory area. It doesn't actually own the memory, but it can read and change its content (it is a *view*). By using typed memoryviews we can interact with both C and NumPy arrays in the same way.

Memoryviews can be defined using a special syntax. We can define a memoryview of int and a 2D memoryview of double in the following way:

```
cdef int[:] a
cdef double[:, :] b
```

The same syntax applies to function definitions, class attributes, and so on. Any object that exposes a buffer interface will automatically be bound to the memoryview. We can bind the memoryview to an array by the following simple assignment:

```
import numpy as np

cdef int[:] arr
arr_np = np.zeros(10, dtype='int32')
arr = arr_np # We bind the array to the memoryview
```

The new memoryview will share the data with the NumPy array. Changes in the array elements will be shared between the two data structures:

```
arr[2] = 1 # Changing memoryview
print(arr_np)
# [0 0 1 0 0 0 0 0 0 0]
```

In a certain sense, the memoryview is a generalization of a NumPy array. As we have seen in *Chapter 2, Fast Array Operations with Numpy*, slicing a NumPy array does not copy the data but returns a view on the same memory area.

Memoryviews also support array slicing with the following standard NumPy syntax:

```
cdef int[:, :, :] a
arr[0, :, :] # Is a 2-dimensional memoryview
arr[0, 0, :] # Is a 1-dimensional memoryview
arr[0, 0, 0] # Is an int
```

To copy data between a memoryview and another, you can use a syntax similar to the slice assignment, as shown in the following code:

```python
import numpy as np

cdef double[:, :] b
cdef double[:] r
b = np.random.rand(10, 3)
r = np.zeros(3, dtype='float64')

b[0, :] = r # Copy the value of r in the first row of b
```

In the next section, we will use the typed memoryviews to handle the arrays in our particle simulator application.

Particle simulator in Cython

Now that we have a basic understanding on how Cython works we can rewrite the `ParticleSimulator.evolve` method. Thanks to Cython, we can convert our loops in C, thus removing the overhead introduced by the Python interpreter.

In *Chapter 2, Fast Array Operations with Numpy*, we wrote a fairly efficient version of the `evolve` method using NumPy. We can rename the old version as `evolve_numpy` to differentiate it from the new version:

```python
def evolve_numpy(self, dt):
    timestep = 0.00001
    nsteps = int(dt/timestep)

    r_i = np.array([[p.x, p.y] for p in self.particles])
    ang_speed_i = np.array([p.ang_speed for p
      in self.particles])
    v_i = np.empty_like(r_i)

    for i in range(nsteps):
      norm_i = np.sqrt((r_i ** 2).sum(axis=1))

      v_i = r_i[:, [1, 0]]
      v_i[:, 0] *= -1
      v_i /= norm_i[:, np.newaxis]

      d_i = timestep * ang_speed_i[:, np.newaxis] * v_i

      r_i += d_i

    for i, p in enumerate(self.particles):
      p.x, p.y = r_i[i]
```

We want to convert this code to Cython. Our strategy will be to take advantage of the fast indexing operations by removing the NumPy array broadcasting, thus reverting to an indexing-based algorithm. Since Cython generates efficient C code, we are free to use as many loops as we like without any performance penalty.

As a design choice, we can decide to encapsulate the loop in a function that we will rewrite in a Cython module called `cevolve.pyx`. The module will contain a single Python function `c_evolve` that will take the particle positions, the angular velocities, the timestep, and the number of steps as input.

At first, we are not adding typing information; we just want to isolate the function and make sure that we can compile our module without errors.

```python
# file: simul.py
# ... other code
  def evolve_cython(self, dt):
    timestep = 0.00001
    nsteps = int(dt/timestep)

    r_i = np.array([[p.x, p.y] for p in self.particles])
    ang_speed_i = np.array([p.ang_speed for
      p in self.particles])

    c_evolve(r_i, ang_speed_i, timestep, nsteps)

    for i, p in enumerate(self.particles):
      p.x, p.y = r_i[i]

# file: cevolve.pyx
import numpy as np

def c_evolve(r_i, ang_speed_i, timestep, nsteps):
  v_i = np.empty_like(r_i)

  for i in range(nsteps):
    norm_i = np.sqrt((r_i ** 2).sum(axis=1))

    v_i = r_i[:, [1, 0]]
    v_i[:, 0] *= -1
    v_i /= norm_i[:, np.newaxis]

    d_i = timestep * ang_speed_i[:, np.newaxis] * v_i

    r_i += d_i
```

Notice that we don't need a return value for `c_evolve`, as values are updated in the `r_i` array in-place. We can benchmark the untyped Cython version against the old NumPy version by slightly changing our benchmark function, as follows:

```python
def benchmark(npart=100, method='python'):
    particles = [Particle(uniform(-1.0, 1.0),
        uniform(-1.0, 1.0),
        uniform(-1.0, 1.0))
        for i in range(npart)]

    simulator = ParticleSimulator(particles)
    if method=='python':
        simulator.evolve_python(0.1)

    if method == 'cython':
        simulator.evolve_cython(0.1)

    elif method == 'numpy':
        simulator.evolve_numpy(0.1)
```

We can time the different versions in an IPython shell:

```
In [4]: %timeit benchmark(100, 'cython')
1 loops, best of 3: 401 ms per loop
In [5]: %timeit benchmark(100, 'numpy')
1 loops, best of 3: 413 ms per loop
```

The two versions have the same speed. Compiling the Cython module without static typing doesn't have any advantage over pure Python. The next step, is to declare the type of all the important variables so that Cython can perform its optimizations.

We can start by adding types to the function arguments. We will declare the arrays as typed memoryviews containing `double` values. It is worth mentioning that if we pass an array of `int` or `float32` type, the casting won't happen automatically and we would get an error.

```python
def c_evolve(double[:, :] r_i, double[:] ang_speed_i,
    double timestep, int nsteps):
```

At that point, we want to rewrite the loops over the particles and time steps. We can declare the iteration variables `i`, `j` and the particle number `nparticles` as `int`:

```python
cdef int i, j
cdef int nparticles = r_i.shape[0]
```

At this point the algorithm is very similar to the pure Python version; we iterate over the particles and time steps and we compute the velocity and displacement vectors for each particle coordinate, using the following code:

```python
for i in range(nsteps):
    for j in range(nparticles):
        x = r_i[j, 0]
        y = r_i[j, 1]
```

```
ang_speed = ang_speed_i[j]

norm = sqrt(x ** 2 + y ** 2)

vx = (-y)/norm
vy = x/norm

dx = timestep * ang_speed * vx
dy = timestep * ang_speed * vy

r_i[j, 0] += dx
r_i[j, 1] += dy
```

In the previous code, we added the x, y, ang_speed, norm, vx, vy, dx, and dy variables. To avoid the Python interpreter overhead we have to declare them with their corresponding types at the beginning of the function as follows:

```
cdef double norm, x, y, vx, vy, dx, dy, ang_speed
```

We also used a function called sqrt to calculate the norm. If we use the sqrt present in the math module or the one in numpy, we would again include a slow Python function in our critical loop, thus killing our performance. A fast sqrt is available in the standard C library, already wrapped in the libc.math Cython module:

```
from libc.math cimport sqrt
```

After recompiling, we can re-run our benchmark to assess our improvements, as follows:

```
In [4]: %timeit benchmark(100, 'cython')
100 loops, best of 3: 13.4 ms per loop
In [5]: %timeit benchmark(100, 'numpy')
1 loops, best of 3: 429 ms per loop
```

For small particle numbers the speed-up is massive, we obtained a 40x performance improvement over the previous version. However, we should also try with a larger number of particles to test the performance scaling, as in the following code:

```
In [2]: %timeit benchmark(1000, 'cython')
10 loops, best of 3: 134 ms per loop
In [3]: %timeit benchmark(1000, 'numpy')
1 loops, best of 3: 877 ms per loop
```

As we increase the number of particles, the two versions get closer in speed. By increasing the particle size to 1000 we already decreased our speed-up to a more modest 6x. This is likely due to the fact that as we increase the number of particles the Python for-loop overhead gets less and less significant compared to the speed of the other operations.

Profiling Cython

Cython gives us a wonderful tool to quickly find the slow spots due to the Python interpreter—a feature called *annotated view*. We can turn on this feature by compiling a Cython file with the -a option, using the following command line. Cython will generate a HTML file containing our code annotated with some useful information:

```
$ cython -a cevolve.pyx
$ google-chrome cevolve.html
```

The HTML file displayed in the following screenshot shows our Cython file line-by-line:

```
Generated by Cython 0.19.1 on Fri Nov 8 21:13:00 2013

Raw output: cevolve.c

 1: import numpy as np
 2: cimport cython
 3: from libc.math cimport sqrt
 4:
 5: def c_evolve(double[:, :] r_i,double[:] ang_speed_i,
 6:              double timestep,int nsteps):
 7:     cdef int i
 8:     cdef int j
 9:     cdef int nparticles = r_i.shape[0]
10:     cdef double norm, x, y, vx, vy, ang_speed
11:
12:
13:     for i in range(nsteps):
14:         for j in range(nparticles):
15:             x = r_i[j, 0]
16:             y = r_i[j, 1]
17:             ang_speed = ang_speed_i[j]
18:
19:             norm = sqrt(x ** 2 + y ** 2)
20:
21:             vx = (-y)/norm
22:             vy = x/norm
    /* "cevolve.pyx":22
     *
     *         vx = (-y)/norm
     *         vy = x/norm           # <<<<<<<<<<<<<<<
     *
     *         dx = timestep * ang_speed * vx
     */
        if (unlikely(__pyx_v_norm == 0)) {
          #ifdef WITH_THREAD
          PyGILState_STATE __pyx_gilstate_save = PyGILState_Ensure();
          #endif
          PyErr_Format(PyExc_ZeroDivisionError, "float division");
          #ifdef WITH_THREAD
          PyGILState_Release(__pyx_gilstate_save);
          #endif
          {__pyx_filename = __pyx_f[0]; __pyx_lineno = 22; __pyx_clineno = __LINE__; goto __pyx_l
        }
        __pyx_v_vy = (__pyx_v_x / __pyx_v_norm);
23:
24:             dx = timestep * ang_speed * vx
25:             dy = timestep * ang_speed * vy
26:
27:             r_i[j, 0] += dx
28:             r_i[j, 1] += dy
```

Each line has a background color in different shades of yellow; an intense color means that the code has a lot of interpreter-related calls, while white lines gets translated to pure C. Since interpreter calls are typically slow, the objective is to make the function body as white as possible. By clicking on any of the lines we can see the C code generated by the Cython compiler. For example, the line $v\_y = x/norm$ checks that the norm is not 0, raising a `ZeroDivisionError` otherwise. The line `x = r_i[j, 0]` shows that Cython checks that the indexes are within the bounds of the array. You may notice that the last line is of a very intense color, by inspecting the code we can see that this is actually a glitch; the code refers to a boilerplate related to the end of the function.

Cython can shut down those checks to improve speed using its compiler directives. There are three different ways to add compiler directives:

- Using a decorator or a context manager
- Using a comment at the beginning of the file
- Using the Cython command line options

 For a complete list of the Cython compiler directives you can refer to the official documentation at http://docs.cython.org/src/ reference/compilation.html#compiler-directives

For example, to disable the "bounds" checking of arrays, it is sufficient to decorate a function with `cython.boundscheck` in the following way:

```
cimport cython

@cython.boundscheck(False)
def myfunction:
    # Code here
```

We can use `cython.boundscheck` to wrap a block of code into a context manager, as follows:

```
with cython.boundscheck(False):
    # Code here
```

If we want to disable bounds checking for a whole module we can add the following line of code at the beginning of the file:

```
# cython: boundscheck=False
```

To alter the directives with the command line options you can use `-X` as follows:

```
$ cython -X boundscheck=True
```

We can now try to avoid the extra checks in our function by disabling the `boundscheck` directive and enabling `cdivision` (this disables the checks for `ZeroDivisionError`) as in the following code:

```
cimport cython

@cython.boundscheck(False)
@cython.cdivision(True)
def c_evolve(double[:, :] r_i,double[:] ang_speed_i,
    double timestep,int nsteps):
```

If we look at the annotated view again, the loop body is completely white; we removed all traces of the interpreter from the loop. In the following case however, we didn't obtain a performance improvement:

```
In [3]: %timeit benchmark(100, 'cython')
100 loops, best of 3: 13.4 ms per loop
```

We can profile Cython code with `cProfile` by including the `profile=True` directive in our files. To show its usage we can write a function that calculates the Chebyshev distance between two arrays of coordinates. Create a file `cheb.py`:

```
import numpy as np
from distance import chebyshev

def benchmark():
  a = np.random.rand(100, 2)
  b = np.random.rand(100, 2)
  for x1, y1 in a:
    for x2, y2 in b:
      chebyshev(x1, x2, y1, y2)
```

If we try profiling this script as-is, we won't get any statistics regarding the functions that we implemented in Cython. If we want to know the profile metrics for the `max` and `min` functions we have to add the `profile=True` option to the `mathlib.pyx` file, as shown in the following code:

```
# cython: profile=True

cdef int max(int a, int b):
  # Code here
```

We can now profile our script with `%prun` using IPython, as follows:

```
In [2]: import cheb
In [3]: %prun cheb.benchmark()
     2000005 function calls in 2.066 seconds

  Ordered by: internal time

  ncalls tottime percall cumtime percall filename:lineno(function)
     1   1.664   1.664   2.066   2.066 cheb.py:4(benchmark)
1000000   0.351   0.000   0.401   0.000 {distance.chebyshev}
1000000   0.050   0.000   0.050   0.000 mathlib.pyx:2(max)
     2   0.000   0.000   0.000   0.000 {method 'rand' of
       'mtrand.RandomState' objects}
     1   0.000   0.000   2.066   2.066 <string>:1(<module>)
     1   0.000   0.000   0.000   0.000 {method 'disable' of
       '_lsprof.Profiler' objects}
```

From the output, we can see that the `max` function is present and is not a bottleneck. The problem seems to be lying in the `benchmark` function; the issue is likely to be the Python for-loop overhead. In this case, the best strategy would be rewriting the loop in NumPy or port the code to Cython.

Summary

Cython will bring the speed of your programs to another level. Cython programs are much easier to maintain in comparison to C, thanks to the tight integration with Python and the availability of profiling tools.

In this chapter, we introduced the basics of the Cython language and how to make our programs faster by adding static types. We also learned how to work with C arrays, NumPy arrays, and memoryviews.

We optimized our particle simulator by rewriting the critical `evolve` function, obtaining a tremendous speed gain. Finally, we learned how to use the annotated view to quickly spot interpreter related calls and how to enable `cProfile` for Cython scripts.

In the next chapter, we will learn the parallel processing basics and see how to write Python programs that take advantage of multiple processors so that you can write faster programs and solve larger problems.

4

Parallel Processing

With parallel processing you can increase the amount of calculations your program can do in a given time without needing a faster processor. The main idea is to divide a task into many sub-units and employ multiple processors to solve them independently.

CPUs containing several cores (2, 4, 6, 8, ...) have become a common trend in technology. Increasing the speed of a single processor is costly and problematic; while leveraging the parallel capabilities of cheaper multi-core processors is a feasible route to increase performance.

Parallel processing lets you tackle large scale problems. Scientists and engineers commonly run parallel code on supercomputers — huge networks of standard processors — to simulate massive systems. Parallel techniques can also take advantage of graphics chips (a hardware optimized for parallelization).

Python can be used in all of these domains, allowing us to apply parallel processing to all sorts of problems with simplicity and elegance, opening the door to infinite possibilities.

In this chapter, we will:

- Briefly introduce the fundamentals of parallel processing
- Illustrate how to parallelize simple problems with the multiprocessing Python library
- Learn how to write programs with the **IPython parallel** framework
- Further optimize our program using multithreading with Cython and OpenMP

Introduction to parallel programming

In order to parallelize a program, we need to divide the problem into sub-units that can run independently (or almost independently) from each other.

A problem where the sub-units are totally independent from each other is called **embarrassingly parallel**. An element-wise operation on an array is a typical example — the operation needs only to know the element it is handling at the moment. Another example, is our particle simulator — since there are no interactions, each particle can evolve in time independently from the others. Embarrassingly parallel problems are very easy to implement and they perform optimally on parallel architectures.

Other problems may be divided into sub-units but have to share some data to perform their calculations. In those cases, the implementation is less straightforward and can lead to performance issues because of the communication costs.

We will illustrate the concept with an example. Imagine you have a particle simulator, but this time the particles attract other particles within a certain distance (as shown in the following figure). To parallelize this problem we divide the simulation box in regions and assign each region to a different processor. If we evolve the system for one step, some particles will interact with particles in a neighboring region. To perform the next iteration, the new particle positions of the neighboring region are required:

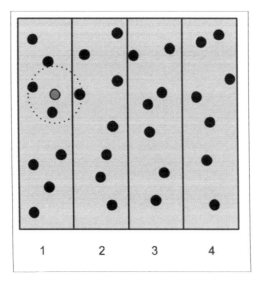

Communication between processes is costly and can seriously hinder the performance of parallel programs. There exists two main ways to handle data communication in parallel programs:

- **Shared memory**
- **Distributed memory**

In shared memory, the sub-units have access to the same memory space. The advantage of this approach, is that you don't have to explicitly handle the communication as it is sufficient to write or read from the shared memory. However, problems arise when multiple processes try to access and change the same memory location at the same time. Care should be taken to avoid such conflict using synchronization techniques.

In the distributed memory model each process is completely separated from the others and possesses its own memory space. In this case, communication is handled explicitly between the processes. The communication overhead is typically costlier compared to shared memory, as data can potentially travel through a network interface.

One common way to achieve parallelism with the shared memory model is **threads**. Threads are independent sub-tasks that originate from a process and share resources such as memory.

Python can spawn and handle threads, but they can't be used to increase performance due to the Python interpreter design—only one Python instruction is allowed to run at a time. This mechanism is called **Global Interpreter Lock (GIL)**. What happens is that, each time a thread executes a Python statement, a lock is acquired which prevents other threads to run until it is released. The GIL avoids conflicts between threads, simplifying the implementation of the **CPython** interpreter. Despite this limitation, threads can still be used to provide concurrency in situations where the lock can be released, such as in time-consuming I/O operations or in C extensions.

The GIL can be completely avoided by using processes instead of threads. Processes don't share the same memory area and are independent from each other—each process has its own interpreter. By using processes, we'll have very few disadvantages: inter-process communication is less efficient than shared memory, but it is more flexible and explicit.

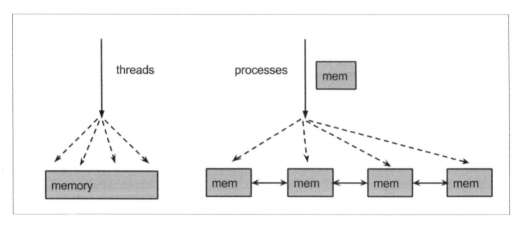

The multiprocessing module

The standard `multiprocessing` module can be used to quickly parallelize simple tasks by spawning several processes. Its interface is easy-to-use and includes several utilities to handle task submission and synchronization.

The Process and Pool classes

You can create a process that runs independently by subclassing `multiprocessing.Process`. You can extend the `__init__` method to initialize resources and you can write the portion of the code destined to the subprocess by implementing a `Process.run` method. In the following code, we define a process that will wait for one second and print its assigned `id`:

```
import multiprocessing
import time

class Process(multiprocessing.Process):
    def __init__(self, id):
```

```
        super(Process, self).__init__()
        self.id = id

    def run(self):
        time.sleep(1)
        print("I'm the process with id: {}".format(self.id))
```

To spawn the process, we have to initialize our `Process` object and call the `Process.start` method. Notice that you don't directly call `Process.run`: the call to `Process.start` will create a new process and, in turn, call the `Process.run` method. We can add the following lines at the end of the script to initialize and start the new process:

```
if __name__ == '__main__':
    p = Process(0)
    p.start()
```

The instructions after `Process.start` will be executed immediately without waiting for the process p to finish. To wait for the task completion you can use the method `Process.join`, as follows:

```
if __name__ == '__main__':
    p = Process(0)
    p.start()
    p.join()
```

We can launch in the same way four different processes that will run in parallel. In a serial program, the total required time would be four seconds. Since we run it parallelly, each process will run at the same time, resulting in a 1-second wallclock time. In the following code, we create four processes and start them parallelly:

```
if __name__ == '__main__':
    processes = Process(1), Process(2), Process(3), Process(4)
    [p.start() for p in processes]
```

Notice that the order of the execution of parallel processes is unpredictable, it ultimately depends on how the operating system schedules the process execution. You can verify this behavior by running the program multiple times—the order will be different at each run.

The `multiprocessing` module exposes a convenient interface that makes it easy to assign and distribute tasks to a set of processes, the `multiprocessing.Pool` class.

The `multiprocessing.Pool` class spawns a set of processes — called **workers** — and lets submit tasks through the methods `apply`/`apply_async` and `map`/`map_async`.

The `Pool.map` method applies a function to each element of a list and returns the list of results. Its usage is equivalent to the built-in (serial) `map`.

To use a parallel map, you should first initialize a `multiprocessing.Pool` object. It takes the number of workers as its first argument; if not provided, that number will be equal to the number of cores in the system. You can initialize a `multiprocessing.Pool` object in the following way:

```
pool = multiprocessing.Pool()
pool = multiprocessing.Pool(processes=4)
```

Let's see `Pool.map` in action. If you have a function that computes the square of a number, you can map the function to the list by calling `Pool.map` and passing the function and the list of inputs as arguments, as follows:

```
def square(x):
    return x * x

inputs = [0, 1, 2, 3, 4]
outputs = pool.map(square, inputs)
```

The `Pool.map_async` method is just like `Pool.map` but returns an `AsyncResult` object instead of the actual result. When we call the normal `map`, the execution of the main program is stopped until all the workers are finished processing the result. With `map_async`, the `AsyncResult` object is returned immediately without blocking the main program and the calculations are done in the background. We can then retrieve the result by using the `AsyncResult.get` method at any time, as shown in the following lines:

```
outputs_async = pool.map_async(square, inputs)
outputs = outputs_async.get()
```

`Pool.apply_async` assigns a task consisting of a single function to one of the workers. It takes the function and its arguments and returns an `AsyncResult` object. We can obtain an effect similar to `map` by using `apply_async`, as shown in the following code:

```
results_async = [pool.apply_async(square, i) for i in range(100))]
results = [r.get() for r in results_async]
```

As an example, we will implement a canonical, embarassingly parallel program: the **Monte Carlo approximation of pi**.

Monte Carlo approximation of pi

Imagine we have a square with a side length of 2 units; its area will be 4 units. Now, we inscribe a circle with a radius 1 unit in this square, the area of the circle will be `pi * r^2`. By substituting the value of `r` in the previous equation we get that the numerical value for the area of the circle is `pi * (1)^2 = pi`. You can refer to the following figure for a graphical representation.

If we shoot a lot of random points on this figure, some points will fall into the circle — we'll call them **hits** — while the remaining points — **misses** — will be outside the circle. The idea of the Monte Carlo method is that the area of the circle will be proportional to the number of hits, while the area of the square will be proportional to the total number of shots. To get the value of `pi`, it is sufficient to divide the area of the circle (equal to `pi`) by the area of the square (equal to 4) and solve for `pi`:

```
hits/total = area_circle/area_square = pi/4
pi = 4 * hits/total
```

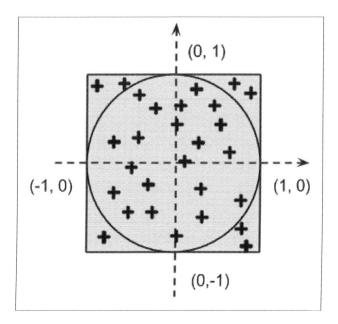

The strategy we will employ in our program will be:

- Generate a lot of sample (x, y) numbers in the range $(-1, 1)$
- Test if those numbers lie inside the circle by checking if `x**2 + y**2 == 1`

We first write a serial version and check if it works. Then, we can write the parallel version. The implementation of the serial program is as follows:

```
import random

samples = 1000000
hits = 0

for i in range(samples):
    x = random.uniform(-1.0, 1.0)
    y = random.uniform(-1.0, 1.0)

    if x**2 + y**2 <= 1:
        hits += 1

pi = 4.0 * hits/samples
```

The accuracy of our approximation will improve as we increase the number of samples. You can notice that each loop iteration is independent from the other—this problem is embarassingly parallel.

To parallelize this code, we can write a function called `sample` that corresponds to a single hit-miss check. If the sample hits the circle, the function will return `1`; otherwise it will return `0`. By running `sample` multiple times and summing the results, we'll get the total number of hits. We can run `sample` over multiple processors with `apply_async` and get the results in the following way:

```
def sample():
    x = random.uniform(-1.0, 1.0)
    y = random.uniform(-1.0, 1.0)

    if x**2 + y**2 <= 1:
        return 1
    else:
        return 0

pool = multiprocessing.Pool()
results_async = [pool.apply_async(sample) for i in range(samples)]
hits = sum(r.get() for r in results_async)
```

We can wrap the two versions in the functions `pi_serial` and `pi_apply_async` (you can find their implementation in the `pi.py` file) and benchmark the execution speed as follows:

```
$ time python -c 'import pi; pi.pi_serial()'
real    0m0.734s
user    0m0.731s
sys     0m0.004s
$ time python -c 'import pi; pi.pi_apply_async()'
real    1m36.989s
user    1m55.984s
sys     0m50.386
```

As shown in the previous benchmark, our first parallel version literally cripples our code. The reason is that the time spent doing the actual calculation is small compared to the overhead required to send and distribute the tasks to the workers.

To solve the issue, we have to make the overhead negligible compared to the calculation time. For example, we can ask each worker to handle more than one sample at a time, thus reducing the task communication overhead. We can write a function `sample_multiple` that processes more than one hit and modifies our parallel version by splitting our problem in 10, more intensive tasks as shown in the following code:

```
def sample_multiple(samples_partial):
    return sum(sample() for i in range(samples_partial))

ntasks = 10
chunk_size = int(samples/ntasks)
pool = multiprocessing.Pool()
results_async = [pool.apply_async(sample_multiple, chunk_size)
                 for i in range(ntasks)]
hits = sum(r.get() for r in results_async)
```

We can wrap this in a function called `pi_apply_async_chunked` and run it as follows:

```
$ time python -c 'import pi; pi.pi_apply_async_chunked()'
real    0m0.325s
user    0m0.816s
sys     0m0.008s
```

The results are much better; we more than doubled the speed of our program. You can also notice that the user metric is larger than real: the total CPU time is larger than the total time because more than one CPU worked at the same time. If you increase the number of samples, you will notice that the ratio of communication to calculation decreases, giving even better speedups.

Everything is nice and simple when dealing with embarassingly parallel problems. But sometimes, you have to share data between processes.

Synchronization and locks

Even if multiprocessing uses processes (with their own independent memory), it lets you define certain variables and arrays as shared memory. You can define a shared variable by using multiprocessing.Value passing its data type as a string (i integer, d double, f float, and so on). You can update the content of the variable through the value attribute, as shown in the following code snippet:

```
shared_variable = multiprocessing.Value('f')
shared_variable.value = 0
```

When using shared memory, you should be aware of concurrent accesses. Imagine you have a shared integer variable and each process increments its value multiple times. You would define a process class as follows:

```
class Process(multiprocessing.Process):

    def __init__(self, counter):
        super(Process, self).__init__()
        self.counter = counter

    def run(self):
        for i in range(1000):
            self.counter.value += 1
```

You can initialize the shared variable in the main program and pass it to 4 processes, as shown in the following code:

```
def main():
    counter = multiprocessing.Value('i', lock=True)
    counter.value = 0

    processes = [Process(counter) for i in range(4)]
    [p.start() for p in processes]
    [p.join() for p in processes] # processes are done
    print(counter.value)
main()
```

If you run this program (`shared.py` in the code directory) you will notice that the final value of `counter` is not 4000, but it has random values (on my machine they are between 2000 and 2500). If we assume that the arithmetic is correct, we can conclude that there's a problem with the parallelization.

What happens is that multiple processes are trying to access the same shared variable at the same time. The situation is best explained by looking at the following figure. In a serial execution, the first process reads (the number 0), increments it, and writes the new value (1); the second process reads the new value (1), increments it, and writes it again (2). In the parallel execution, the two processes read the value (0), increment it, and write it (1) at the same time, leading to a wrong answer.

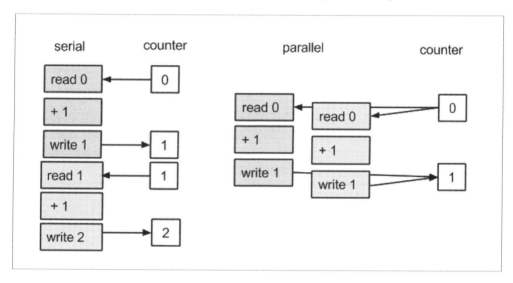

To solve this problem, we need to synchronize the access to this variable so that only one process at a time can access, increment, and write the value on the shared variable. This feature is provided by the `multiprocessing.Lock` class. A lock can be acquired and released through the `acquire` and `release` methods, or by using the lock as a context manager. When a process acquires a lock, other processes are prevented to acquire it until the lock is released.

We can define a global lock, and use it as a context manager to restrict the access to the counter, as shown in the following code snippet:

```
lock = multiprocessing.Lock()

class Process(multiprocessing.Process):
```

```
def __init__(self, counter):
    super(Process, self).__init__()
    self.counter = counter

def run(self):
    for i in range(1000):
        with lock: # acquire the lock
            self.counter.value += 1
        # release the lock
```

Synchronization primitives such as locks are essential to solve many problems but you should avoid overusing them because they can decrease the performance of your program.

 multiprocessing includes other communication and synchronization tools, you can refer to the official documentation for a complete reference:

http://docs.python.org/3/library/multiprocessing.html

IPython parallel

IPython's power is not limited to its advanced shell. Its `parallel` package includes a framework to setup and run calculations on single and multi-core machines, as well as on multiple nodes connected to a network. IPython is great because it gives an interactive twist to parallel computing and provides a common interface to different communication protocols.

To use `IPython.parallel`, you have to start a set of workers — **Engines** — that are managed by a **Controller** (an entity that mediates the communication between the client and the engines). The approach is totally different from multiprocessing; you start the worker processes separately, and they will wait indefinitely, listening for commands from the client.

To start the controller and a set of engines (by default, one engine per processing unit) you can use the `ipcluster` shell command, as follows:

`$ ipcluster start`

With `ipcluster` you can also set up multiple nodes to distribute your calculations over a network by writing a custom profile. You can refer to the official documentation for specific instructions at the following website:

http://ipython.org/ipython-doc/dev/parallel/parallel_process.html

After starting the controller and the engines, we can use an IPython shell to perform calculations in parallel. IPython provides two basic interfaces (or views): **direct** and **task-based**.

Direct interface

The direct interface lets you issue commands explicitly to each of the computing units. The interface is intuitive, flexible, and easy-to-use, especially when used in an interactive session.

After starting the engines, you have to start an IPython session in a separate shell to interact with them. By creating a client, you can establish a connection to the controller. In the following code, we import the `Client` class and create an instance:

```
In [1]: from IPython.parallel import Client
In [2]: rc = Client()
```

The attribute `Client.ids` will give you a list of integers representing the available engines, as shown in the following code snippet:

```
In [3]: rc.ids
Out[4]: [0, 1, 2, 3]
```

We can issue commands to the engines by obtaining a `DirectView` instance. You can get a `DirectView` instance by either indexing the `Client` instance or by calling the `DirectView.direct_view` method. The following code shows different ways to obtain a `DirectView` instance from the previously created `Client`:

```
In [5]: dview = rc[0] # Select the first engine
In [6]: dview = rc[::2] # Select every other engine
In [7]: dview = rc[:] # Selects all the engines
In [8]: dview = rc.direct_view('all') # Alternative
```

You can treat the engines like fresh IPython sessions. At the finest level, you can execute commands remotely by using the `DirectView.execute` method:

```
In [9]: dview.execute('a = 1')
```

The command will be sent and executed individually by each engine. The return value will be an `AsyncResult` object and the actual return value can be retrieved using the `get` method.

As shown in the following code, you can retrieve the data contained in a remote variable by using the `DirectView.pull` method and send the data to a remote variable with the `DirectView.push` method. The `DirectView` class also supports a convenient dictionary-like interface:

```
In [10]: dview.pull('a').get() # equivalent: dview['a']
Out[10]: [1, 1, 1, 1]
In [11]: dview.push({'a': 2}) # equivalent: dview['a'] = 2
```

It is possible to send and retrieve every object that can be serialized using the `pickle` module. On top of that, special handling is reserved for data structures such as **NumPy** arrays to increase the efficiency.

If you issue a statement that causes an exception, you will receive a summary of the exceptions in each engine:

```
In [12]: res = dview.execute('a = *__*') # Invalid
In [13]: res.get()
[0:execute]:
   File "<ipython-input-3-945a473d5cbb>", line 1
     a = *__*
           ^
SyntaxError: invalid syntax

[1:execute]:
   File "<ipython-input-3-945a473d5cbb>", line 1
     a = *__*
           ^
SyntaxError: invalid syntax
[2: execute]:
...
```

Engines should be treated as independent IPython sessions, and imports and custom-defined functions must be synchronized over the network. To import some libraries, both locally and in the engines, you can use the `DirectView.sync_imports` context manager:

```
with dview.sync_imports():
    import numpy
    # The syntax import _ as _ is not supported
```

To submit calculations to the engines, `DirectView` provides some utilities for common use cases such as map and apply. The `DirectView.map` method works similarly to `Pool.map_async`, as shown in the following code snippet. You map a function to a sequence, returning an `AsyncResult` object

```
In [14]: a = range(100)
In [15]: def square(x): return x * x
In [16]: result_async = dview.map(square, a)
In [17]: result = result_async.get()
```

IPython provides a more convenient map implementation through the `DirectView.parallel` decorator. If you apply the decorator on a function, the function will now have a `map` method that can be applied to a sequence. In the following code, we apply the parallel decorator to the `square` function and map it over a series of numbers:

```
In [18]: @dview.parallel()
    ...: def square(x):
    ...:     return x * x
In [19]: square.map(range(100))
```

 To get the non-blocking version of map, you can either use the `DirectView.map_sync` method or pass the `block=True` option to the `DirectView.parallel` decorator.

The `DirectView.apply` method behaves in a different way than `Pool.apply_async`. The function gets executed on *every* engine. For example, if we have selected four engines and we apply the `square` function, the function gets executed once per engine and it returns four results, as shown in the following code snippet:

```
In [20]: def square(x):
             return x * x
In [21]: result_async = dview.apply(square, 2)
In [22]: result_async.get()
Out[22]: [4, 4, 4, 4]
```

The `DirectiView.remote` decorator lets you create a function that will run directly on each engine. Its usage is as follows:

```
In [23]: @dview.remote()
    ...: def square(x):
    ...:     return x * x
    ...:
In [24]: square(2)
Out[24]: [4, 4, 4, 4]
```

The `DirectView` also provides two other kinds of communication scheme: **scatter** and **gather**.

Scatter distributes a list of inputs to the engines. Imagine you have four inputs and four engines; you can distribute those inputs in a remote variable with `DirectView.scatter`, as follows:

```
In [25]: dview.scatter('a', [0, 1, 2, 3])
In [26]: dview['a']
Out[26]: [[0], [1], [2], [3]]
```

Scatter will try to distribute the inputs as equally as possible even when the number of inputs is not a multiple of the number of engines. The following code shows how a list of 11 computations gets processed in three batches of three items per batch and one batch of two items:

```
In [13]: dview.scatter('a', [0, 1, 2, 3, 4, 5, 6, 7, 8, 9, 10])
In [14]: dview['a']
Out[14]: [[0, 1, 2], [3, 4, 5], [6, 7, 8], [9, 10]]
```

The gather function simply retrieves the scattered values and merges them back. In the following snippet, we merge back the scattered results:

```
In [17]: dview.gather('a').get()
Out[17]: [0, 1, 2, 3, 4, 5, 6, 7, 8, 9, 10]
```

We can use the scatter and gather functions to parallelize one of our simulations. In our system, each particle is independent from the other, therefore, we can use scatter and gather to divide the particles equally between the available engines, evolve them, and get the particles back from the engines.

At first, we have to set up the engines. The ParticleSimulator class should be made available to all the engines.

Remember that the engines have started in a separate process and the simul module should be importable by them. You can achieve this in two ways:

- By launching ipcluster in the directory, where simul.py is located
- By adding that directory to PYTHONPATH

If you're using the code examples, don't forget to compile the Cython extensions using setup.py.

In the following code, we create the particles and obtain a DirectView instance:

```
from random import uniform
from simul import Particle
from IPython.parallel import Client

particles = [Particle(uniform(-1.0, 1.0),
                      uniform(-1.0, 1.0),
                      uniform(-1.0, 1.0)) for i in range(10000)]
rc = Client()
dview = rc[:]
```

Now, we can scatter the particles to a remote variable `particle_chunk`, perform the particle evolution using `DirectView.execute` and retrieve the particles. We do this using `scatter`, `execute`, and `gather`, as shown in the following code:

```
dview.scatter('particle_chunk', particles, block=True)

dview.execute('from simul import ParticleSimulator')
dview.execute('simulator = ParticleSimulator(particle_chunk)')
dview.execute('simulator.evolve_cython(0.1)')

particles = dview.gather('particle_chunk', block=True)
```

We can now wrap the parallel version and benchmark it against the serial one (refer to the file `simul_parallel.py`) in the following way:

```
In [1]: from simul import benchmark
In [2]: from simul_parallel import scatter_gather
In [5]: %timeit benchmark(10000, 'cython')
1 loops, best of 3: 1.34 s per loop
In [6]: %timeit scatter_gather(10000)
1 loops, best of 3: 720 ms per loop
```

The code is extremely simple and gives us a 2x speedup, scalable on any number of engines.

Task-based interface

IPython has an interface that can handle computing tasks in a smart way. While this implies a less flexible interface from the user point of view, it can improve performance by balancing the load on the engines and by re-submitting failed jobs. In this section, we will introduce the `map` and `apply` functions in the task-based interface.

The task interface is provided by the `LoadBalancedView` class, which can be obtained from a client using the `load_balanced_view` method, as follows:

```
In [1]: from IPython.parallel import Client
In [2]: rc = Client()
In [3]: tview = rc.load_balanced_view()
```

At this point we can run some tasks using `map` and `apply`. The `LoadBalancedView` class works similarly to `multiprocessing.Pool`, the tasks are submitted and handled by a scheduler; in the case of `LoadBalancedView`, the task assignment is based on how much load is present on an engine at a given time, ensuring that all the engines are working without downtimes.

It's helpful to explain an important difference between `apply` in `DirectView` and `LoadBalancedView`. A call to `DirectView.apply` will run on *every* selected engine, while a call to `LoadBalancedView.apply` will schedule a *single* task to one of the engines. In the first case, the result will be a list, and in the latter, it will be a single value, as shown in the following code snippet:

```
In [4]: dview = rc[:]
In [5]: tview = rc.load_balanced_view()
In [6]: def square(x):
   ...:         return x * x
   ...:
In [7]: dview.apply(square, 2).get()
Out[7]: [4, 4, 4, 4]
In [8]: tview.apply(square, 2).get()
Out[8]: 4
```

`LoadBalancedView` is also able to handle failures and run tasks on engines when certain conditions are met. This feature is provided through a dependency system. We will not cover this aspect in this book, but interested readers can refer to the official documentation at the following link:

`http://ipython.org/ipython-doc/rel-1.1.0/parallel/parallel_task.html`

Parallel Cython with OpenMP

Cython provides a convenient interface to perform shared-memory parallel processing through **OpenMP**. This lets you write extremely efficient parallel code directly in Cython without having to create a C wrapper.

OpenMP is a specification to write multithreaded programs, and includes series of C preprocessor directives to manage threads; these include communication patterns, load balancing, and synchronization features. Several C/C++ and Fortran compilers (including GCC) implement the OpenMP API.

Let's introduce Cython parallel features with a small example. Cython provides a simple API based on OpenMP in the `cython.parallel` module. The simplest construct is `prange`: a construct that automatically distributes loop operations in multiple threads.

First of all, we can write a serial version of a program that computes the square of each element of a NumPy array in the `hello_parallel.pyx` file. We get a buffer as input and we create an output array by populating it with the squares of the input array elements.

The serial version, `square_serial`, is shown in the following code snippet:

```
import numpy as np

def square_serial(double[:] inp):
    cdef int i, size
    cdef double[:] out
    size = inp.shape[0]
    out_np = np.empty(size, 'double')
    out = out_np

    for i in range(size):
        out[i] = inp[i]*inp[i]

    return out_np
```

Now, we can change the loop in a parallel version by substituting the range call with `prange`. There's a caveat, you need to make sure that the body of the loop is interpreter-free. As already explained, to make use of threads we need to release the GIL, since interpreter calls acquire and release the GIL, we should avoid them. Failure in doing so will result in compilation errors.

In Cython, you can release the GIL by using `nogil`, as follows:

```
with nogil:
    for i in prange(size):
        out[i] = inp[i]*inp[i]
```

Alternatively, you can use the convenient option `nogil=True` of `prange` that will automatically wrap the loop in a `nogil` block:

```
for i in prange(size, nogil=True):
    out[i] = inp[i]*inp[i]
```

> Attempts to call Python code in a `prange` block results in an error. This includes assignment operations, function calls, objects initialization, and so on. To include such operations in a `prange` block (you may want to do so for debugging purposes) you have to re-enable the GIL using the `with gil` statement:
>
> ```
> for i in prange(size, nogil=True):
>     out[i] = inp[i]*inp[i]
>     with gil:
>         x = 0 # Python assignment
> ```

At this point, we need to recompile our extension. We need to change `setup.py` to enable OpenMP support. You have to specify the GCC option `-fopenmp` using the `Extension` class in `distutils` and pass it to the `cythonize` function. The following code shows the complete `setup.py` file:

```
from distutils.core import setup
from distutils.extension import Extension
from Cython.Build import cythonize

hello_parallel = Extension('hello_parallel',
                           ['hello_parallel.pyx'],
                           extra_compile_args=['-fopenmp'],
                           extra_link_args=['-fopenmp'])

setup(
    name='Hello',
    ext_modules = cythonize(['cevolve.pyx', hello_parallel]),
)
```

Now that we know how to use `prange`, we can quickly parallelize the Cython version of our `ParticleSimulator`.

In the following code, we can take a look at the `c_evolve` function contained in the Cython module `cevolve.pyx` that we wrote in *Chapter 2, Fast Array Operations with NumPy*:

```
def c_evolve(double[:, :] r_i,double[:] ang_speed_i,
             double timestep,int nsteps):

    # cdef declarations

    for i in range(nsteps):
        for j in range(nparticles):
            # loop body
```

The first thing we have to do is invert the order of the loops; we want the outermost loop to be the parallel one, where each iteration is independent from the other. Since the particles don't interact with each other, we can change the order of iteration safely, as shown in the following code snippet:

```
    for j in range(nparticles):
        for i in range(nsteps):

            # loop body
```

At that point we can parallelize the loop using `prange`, we already removed the interpreter-related calls when we added static typing, so the `nogil` block can be applied safely, as follows:

```
for j in prange(nparticles, nogil=True)
```

We can now wrap the two different versions into separate functions and we can time them, as follows:

```
In [3]: %timeit benchmark(10000, 'openmp')
1 loops, best of 3: 599 ms per loop
In [4]: %timeit benchmark(10000, 'cython')
1 loops, best of 3: 1.35 s per loop
```

With OpenMP, we are able to obtain a significant speedup compared to the serial Cython version by changing a single line of code.

Summary

Parallel processing is an effective way to increase the speed of your programs or to handle large amounts of data. Embarassingly parallel problems are excellent candidates for parallelization and lead to a straightforward implementation and optimal scaling.

In this chapter, we illustrated the basics of parallel programming in Python. We learned how to use multiprocessing to easily parallelize programs with the tools already included in Python. Another more powerful tool for parallel processing is IPython parallel. This package allows you to interactively prototype parallel programs and manage a network of computing nodes effectively. Finally, we explored the easy-to-use multithreading capabilities of Cython and OpenMP.

During the course of this book, we learned the most effective techniques to design, benchmark, profile, and optimize Python applications. NumPy can be used to elegantly rewrite Python loops, and if it is not enough, you can use Cython to generate efficient C code. At the last stage, you can easily parallelize your program using the tools presented in this chapter.

Index

Symbols

-v option 15

A

application
  code optimization, steps 8
  designing 7-13
arrays
  accessing 34-37
  C arrays 58-60
  creating 32, 33
  NumPy arrays 60, 61
  pointers 58-60
  typed memoryviews 61-63
  woking with 58
AsyncResult object 76
axes 32

B

benchmarks
  timing 15, 17
  writing 13, 14
bisect module 29
bottlenecks
  searching, cProfile used 17-21
bytecode 25

C

call graph 21
C arrays 58
cdef keyword 52, 55
cell magics 16
cells 16
chebyshev function 57

classes 55, 56
code
  optimizing 23, 24
collections module 28
column-mayor 59
Controller 82
cProfile module
  about 17
  used, for bottlenecks detecting 17-21
CPython interpreter 73
Cython
  about 29, 49
  extensions, compiling 49-51
  particle simulator 63
  profiling 67-70
  with OpenMP 88-91
cython command 50
Cython extensions
  compiling 49-51
cython.parallel module 88

D

declarations
  sharing 56, 57
direct interface, IPython parallel
  DirectiView.remote decorator 85
  DirectView.apply function 85
  DirectView.direct_view method 83
  DirectView.execute 87
  DirectView.map method 84
  DirectView.parallel decorator 85
  DirectView.pull method 83
  DirectView.sync_imports 84
  gather function 86
  ParticleSimulator class 86
  scatter 85

O

OpenMP 88-91
optimal performance
  reaching, with numexpr 45, 46

P

parallel processing 71
parallel programming
  about 72
  communication, handling 73
  distributed memory 73
  shared memory 73
particle simulator
  about 8
  rewriting, in NumPy 41-44
ParticleSimulator class 86
pointers 58
Pool.apply_async 76
Pool.map_async function 76
Pool.map method 76
printf function 58
Process.run method 74, 75
Process.start method 75
profile function 22
profile module 17
profiler 7
profiling 7
pure Python code
  performance tuning tips 28, 29

R

row-major 59

S

scatter 85
shared memory 73
static types
  adding 52
  classes 55, 56
  functions 54, 55
  variables 52-54

T

task-based interface, IPython parallel
  about 87
  DirectView.apply 88
  LoadBalancedView 87, 88
  load_balanced_view method 87
tests
  writing 13, 14
threads 73
throughput 71
time command 15

V

variables 52, 53, 54
visualize function 12

W

workers 76

Thank you for buying
Python High Performance Programming

About Packt Publishing

Packt, pronounced 'packed', published its first book "*Mastering phpMyAdmin for Effective MySQL Management*" in April 2004 and subsequently continued to specialize in publishing highly focused books on specific technologies and solutions.

Our books and publications share the experiences of your fellow IT professionals in adapting and customizing today's systems, applications, and frameworks. Our solution based books give you the knowledge and power to customize the software and technologies you're using to get the job done. Packt books are more specific and less general than the IT books you have seen in the past. Our unique business model allows us to bring you more focused information, giving you more of what you need to know, and less of what you don't.

Packt is a modern, yet unique publishing company, which focuses on producing quality, cutting-edge books for communities of developers, administrators, and newbies alike. For more information, please visit our website: www.packtpub.com.

About Packt Open Source

In 2010, Packt launched two new brands, Packt Open Source and Packt Enterprise, in order to continue its focus on specialization. This book is part of the Packt Open Source brand, home to books published on software built around Open Source licenses, and offering information to anybody from advanced developers to budding web designers. The Open Source brand also runs Packt's Open Source Royalty Scheme, by which Packt gives a royalty to each Open Source project about whose software a book is sold.

Writing for Packt

We welcome all inquiries from people who are interested in authoring. Book proposals should be sent to author@packtpub.com. If your book idea is still at an early stage and you would like to discuss it first before writing a formal book proposal, contact us; one of our commissioning editors will get in touch with you.

We're not just looking for published authors; if you have strong technical skills but no writing experience, our experienced editors can help you develop a writing career, or simply get some additional reward for your expertise.

Python Data Visualization Cookbook

ISBN: 978-1-782163-36-7   Paperback: 280 pages

Over 60 recipes that will enable you to learn how to create attractive visualizations using Python's most popular libraries

1. Learn how to set up an optimal Python environment for data visualization

2. Understand the topics such as importing data for visualization and formatting data for visualization

3. Understand the underlying data and how to use the right visualizations

Python Geospatial Development - Second Edition

ISBN: 978-1-782161-52-3   Paperback: 508 pages

Learn to build sophisticated mapping applications from scratch using Python tools for geospatial development

1. Build your own complete and sophisticated mapping applications in Python.

2. Walks you through the process of building your own online system for viewing and editing geospatial data

3. Practical, hands-on tutorial that teaches you all about geospatial development in Python

Please check **www.PacktPub.com** for information on our titles

OpenCV Computer Vision
with Python

ISBN: 978-1-782163-92-3   Paperback: 122 pages

Learn to capture videos, manipulate images, and
track objects with Python using the OpenCV Library

1. Set up OpenCV, its Python bindings, and
   optional Kinect drivers on Windows, Mac or
   Ubuntu

2. Create an application that tracks and
   manipulates faces

3. Identify face regions using normal color images
   and depth images

Getting Started with Python
Pandas

ISBN: 978-1-782171-24-9   Paperback: 120 pages

An in-depth guide to core the concepts of the Pandas
library, including best practices for data analysis in
Python

1. Understand the core concepts, data structures,
   and algorithms implemented in the Pandas
   library

2. Learn how to acquire, clean, transform, and
   present your data in a scientific manner

3. Experience how easy data analysis is using
   Python and Pandas

Please check **www.PacktPub.com** for information on our titles

Made in the USA
Lexington, KY
18 June 2014